Ann M. Martin

WHO
WROTE
THAT?

WHO WROTE THAT?

Ann M. Martin

Marylou Morano Kjelle

Foreword by
Kyle Zimmer

CHELSEA HOUSE
PUBLISHERS
An imprint of Infobase Publishing

Ann M. Martin

Copyright © 2006 by Infobase Publishing

Chelsea House
An imprint of Infobase Publishing
132 West 31st Street
New York NY 10001

Library of Congress Cataloging-in-Publication Data

Kjelle, Marylou Morano.
  Ann M. Martin / Marylou Morano Kjelle.
    p. cm. — (Who wrote that?)
  Includes bibliographical references and index.
  ISBN 0-7910-8794-8
  1. Martin, Ann M., 1955- 2. Authors, American—20th century—Biography. 3.
Children's literature—Authorship. I. Title. II. Series.
  PS3563.A72322Z74 2005
  813'.54—dc22   2005020414

Chelsea House books are available at special discounts when purchased in bulk quantities for business, associations, institutions, or sales promotions. Please call our Special Sales Department in New York at (212) 967-8800 or (800) 322-8755.

You can find Chelsea House on the World Wide Web at http://www.chelseahouse.com

Text and cover design by Keith Trego

Printed in the United States of America

Bang EJB 10 9 8 7 6 5 4 3 2 1

This book is printed on acid-free paper.

All links and Web addresses were checked and verified to be correct at the time of publication. Because of the dynamic nature of the Web, some addresses and links may have changed since publication and may no longer be valid.

Table of Contents

FOREWORD BY
KYLE ZIMMER
PRESIDENT, FIRST BOOK

HUMANITY IS POWERED by stories. From our earliest days as thinking beings, we employed every available tool to tell each other stories. We danced, drew pictures on the walls of our caves, spoke, and sang. All of this extraordinary effort was designed to entertain, recount the news of the day, explain natural occurrences—and then gradually to build religious and cultural traditions and establish the common bonds and continuity that eventually formed civilizations. Stories are the most powerful force in the universe; they are the primary element that has distinguished our evolutionary path.

Our love of the story has not diminished with time. Enormous segments of societies are devoted to the art of storytelling. Book sales in the United States alone topped $26 billion last year; movie studios spend fortunes to create and promote stories; and the news industry is more pervasive in its presence than ever before.

There is no mystery to our fascination. Great stories are magic. They can introduce us to new cultures, or remind us of the nobility and failures of our own, inspire us to greatness or scare us to death; but above all, stories provide human insight on a level that is unavailable through any other source. In fact, stories connect each of us to the rest of humanity not just in our own time, but also throughout history.

This special magic of books is the greatest treasure that we can hand down from generation to generation. In fact, that spark in a child that comes from books became the motivation for the creation of my organization, First Book, a national literacy program with a simple mission: to provide new books to the most disadvantaged children. At present, First Book has been at work in hundreds of communities for over a decade. Every year children in need receive millions of books through our organization and millions more are provided through dedicated literacy institutions across the United States and around the world. In addition, groups of people dedicate themselves tirelessly to working with children to share reading and stories in every imaginable setting from schools to the streets. Of course, this Herculean effort serves many important goals. Literacy translates to productivity and employability in life and many other valid and even essential elements. But at the heart of this movement are people who love stories, love to read, and want desperately to ensure that no one misses the wonderful possibilities that reading provides.

When thinking about the importance of books, there is an overwhelming urge to cite the literary devotion of great minds. Some have written of the magnitude of the importance of literature. Amy Lowell, an American poet, captured the concept when she said, "Books are more than books. They are the life, the very heart and core of ages past, the reason why men lived and worked and died, the essence and quintessence of their lives." Others have spoken of their personal obsession with books, as in Thomas Jefferson's simple statement: "I live for books." But more compelling, perhaps, is the almost instinctive excitement in children for books and stories.

Throughout my years at First Book, I have heard truly extraordinary stories about the power of books in the lives of children. In one case, a homeless child, who had been bounced from one location to another, later resurfaced—and the only possession that he had fought to keep was the book he was given as part of a First Book distribution months earlier. More recently, I met a child who, upon receiving the book he wanted, flashed a big smile and said, "This is my big chance!" These snapshots reveal the true power of books and stories to give hope and change lives.

As these children grow up and continue to develop their love of reading, they will owe a profound debt to those volunteers who reached out to them—a debt that they may repay by reaching out to spark the next generation of readers. But there is a greater debt owed by all of us—a debt to the storytellers, the authors, who have bound us together, inspired our leaders, fueled our civilizations, and helped us put our children to sleep with their heads full of images and ideas.

WHO WROTE THAT? is a series of books dedicated to introducing us to a few of these incredible individuals. While we have almost always honored stories, we have not uniformly honored storytellers. In fact, some of the most important authors have toiled in complete obscurity throughout their lives or have been openly persecuted for the uncomfortable truths that they have laid before us. When confronted with the magnitude of their written work or perhaps the daily grind of our own, we can forget that writers are people. They struggle through the same daily indignities and dental appointments, and they experience the intense joy and bottomless despair that many of us do. Yet somehow they rise above it all to deliver a powerful thread that connects us all. It is a rare honor to have the opportunity that these books provide to share the lives of these extraordinary people. Enjoy.

Ann M. Martin (right) and Jean Feiwel are shown discussing ideas for the Baby-sitters Club series in 1989 at Scholastic Inc. In 1985, Feiwel had asked Martin to write the first four books of the series and over the years of working together, the two women formed a close friendship.

1

A Series Is Born

KRISTY THOMAS, Mary Anne Spier, Claudia Kishi, and Stacey McGill. Over the years, the antics of these four fictitious seventh graders who called themselves the "Baby-sitters Club," have warmed the hearts of millions of readers and made their creator, Ann M. Martin, one of the most beloved and widely read children's authors of all time.

Martin never intended to have a career as a children's book author. In fact, Martin's career path took her in several directions before her name became synonymous with the best-selling series. But although she did not begin writing seriously until she was 25 years old, Martin's writing talent was evident in grammar school. Her fourth grade teacher, Mrs. Dreeban, wrote in Martin's student folder that she could be a writer, if she wanted to. "She spent a lot of her free time doing her own writing, and what she wrote was beautiful," Mrs. Dreeban later recalled.[1]

Martin, too, remembers her childhood enjoyment of writing. "My favorite subject in school was English because I loved to write. I just didn't know at the time that it would become my profession," she said.[2]

By the time she was in high school, Martin had decided that she would become a teacher. She loved children and wanted to show them that learning could be fun. She also had a unique gift for working with children who were handicapped in some way. As a teenager, she spent summers working at the Eden Institute, a school for autistic children in Princeton, New Jersey. After high school, Martin attended Smith College in Northampton, Massachusetts, where she studied both elementary education and child psychology. Finally, in the fall of 1977, she reached her goal. Her first job after graduation was co-teaching developmentally disabled fourth and fifth graders at a small school in Connecticut.

One of Martin's favorite activities as a teacher was reading to her students and in doing so, she rekindled her passion for children's literature and for writing. After one year, Martin left teaching and took a job in children's publishing. She worked first for Pocket Books, then Scholastic Inc., and eventually for Bantam Books for Young Readers, three well-known and well-established publishers of children's books.

Martin began her career in publishing as an editorial assistant and eventually worked her way up to the position of senior editor. Editors perform many tasks within publishing houses. One of the most important tasks an editor does is finding new books to be published. Each day Martin read dozens of manuscripts sent to her by authors hoping that their work was going to be published. As she read the manuscripts others had written, Martin realized something important about herself. She was as good a writer, if not better, than many of the authors who sent her their work. She knew that she too could write a book. Why didn't she?

In 1980, Martin faced the challenge she had given herself and began writing a book targeted towards middle grade students. She wrote in the early morning hours before going to work at the publishing house and on weekends. Three years later, *Bummer Summer*, the story of a young girl who must deal with her widowed father's remarriage, was published by Holiday House publishers.

Bummer Summer fanned the writing flame that had burned inside of Martin since she was a student in the fourth grade. Once she started writing, she found she could not stop. Still writing in the mornings and on weekends, Martin completed four more books—*Inside Out, Stage Fright, Me and Katie (the Pest)*, and *With or Without You*—in the next few years. All of the books were well-received by young readers and reviewers alike.

By the mid 1980s, Martin's success as a writer forced her to make a decision. How did she see herself? Was she a full-time writer working as an editor, or a full-time editor writing in her free time? Martin chose the former, and in 1985 she struck out on her own as a freelance writer.

Back in 1983, Scholastic Inc. had published a book about a girl who baby-sat. The book sold well, and gave Jean Feiwel—the senior vice president and editor-in-chief at Scholastic Inc.—an idea. Since young readers were interested in stories that focused on the theme of baby-sitting,

Jean thought a fictional series about four friends who form a baby-sitting business might also sell well. Jean titled the series the Baby-sitters Club. "There was something resonant about the idea. It just struck a chord with me," she said.[3]

Jean had read Martin's five published books and had been impressed by them. Because the two women had worked together previously at Scholastic Inc., Jean knew that in addition to being a good writer, Martin was also hard working and dedicated. She was just the person to be trusted with the type of project Jean had in mind. In 1985, Jean offered Martin a contract to write the first four books in the Baby-sitters Club series, and Martin eagerly accepted her offer. Writing the books would bring in enough of an income that Martin would not have to worry about paying her bills for a while. Plus, as a former baby-sitter, Martin had, without question, numerous experiences that she could write about in the books.

The original plan was to write one book about each girl in the Baby-sitters Club. "The [series] title was already chosen, but it was up to me to figure out what it meant and who the characters would be," said Martin.[4] She designed her plots around the escapades of four (later eight) pre-teen girls living in the fictitious suburb of Stoneybrook, Connecticut.

Stoneybrook is written as a safe and secure city, not unlike Princeton, New Jersey, where Martin had grown up. In the Baby-sitters Club books, the girls get together and start a baby-sitting business. They meet three times a week after school and wait for parents who need sitters to call for their services.

Each Baby-sitters Club book contains two plots. The first plot involves a personal challenge faced by one of the members of the club. The book revolves around the adventures of

The Baby-sitters Club series was a huge success and Ann M. Martin became a writing celebrity. Martin is shown here signing autographs for the daughters of her Scholastic Inc. co-workers in June 1989.

that particular baby-sitter, and is written in that girl's voice and from her point of view. All of the members of the baby-sitters club help her overcome the challenge, and the viewpoints of other characters are written either in the "club notebook" or in a letter. The second plot has to do with a baby-sitting dilemma. At the conclusion of the book, both conflicts are resolved, and there is a happy ending.

Jean planned to see how the first four Baby-sitters Club books were received before expanding the series. These four titles—*Kristy's Great Idea, Claudia and the Phantom Phone Calls, The Truth About Stacey,* and *Mary Anne Saves the Day*—were released in 1986. A modest 30,000 copies of each book were published. They sold well enough for Jean to ask Martin to write two more books for the series. When the sixth title, *Kristy's Big Day*, made the B. Dalton's juvenile best seller list in 1987, the Baby-sitters Club series really took off. The four previous books also shot to the top of B. Dalton's juvenile best seller list, and once the series reached book seven, the following Baby-sitters Club books were released with first printings of 250,000 copies.

"It just exploded, the books were really selling well, and [Scholastic] asked me to write an entire year's worth," explained Martin.[5] Almost every Baby-sitters Club book published from number seven on made it to B. Dalton's juvenile best seller list. In the late 1980s, of the 20 books on the list at any given time, it was not unusual for half to be books in the Baby-sitters Club series.

Although the Baby-sitters Club books are fictitious, Martin based many of the stories on incidents that had occurred when she had been the babysitter. "My own experiences as a teenage baby-sitter certainly gave me plenty of material for the BSC books," Martin told her fans in a letter she posted on the Scholastic Books website.[6]

The character of Kristy Thomas, the feisty, outspoken girl who has the original idea to form a baby-sitting club, is based on Martin's best friend, Beth McKeever (now Beth Perkins). Mary Anne Spier, Kristy's shy best friend, is similar in personality to Martin. Martin used the personalities of other girls she knew, as well as members of her own family, to create Claudia Kishi and Stacey McGill, and the other characters that appear throughout the series.

Over time, Martin added characters to the original four Baby-sitters Club members. "Adding Dawn, Jessi, Mallory and Abby to the club made writing the series even more fun," she said on the Scholastic Books web page.[7] Martin was happy to see the Baby-sitters Club grow into a series because it gave her the opportunity to really get to know her characters and their different personalities. She also liked being able to turn to the same characters over and over again. "After a point, I realized the characters began to generate their own plot ideas," Martin said. "That made it easier to write for them.[8]

For the first few years, Martin was the sole author of the Baby-sitters Club books. A very self-disciplined author, she wrote one, and sometimes two books a month. As the series grew, Martin was assigned a team of writers to help her. However, Martin always maintained creative control over the books by writing the outlines of the chapters, and revising the manuscripts as she saw fit.

One reason for the continuing popularity of the Baby-sitters Club books is that they are more than fictional stories about girls who baby-sit. Written for readers 8 to 13 years old, the books portray realistic situations, and the Baby-sitters Club characters have the same concerns as the young people who read about them. Working with her editors, Martin created plots that revolved around many current social issues. Some of the subjects the Baby-sitters Club books focus on are: parents' divorce and remarriage, step siblings, disabilities, racism, death, and illnesses such as diabetes. The way the books address these real topics makes the Baby-sitters Club books favorites among young readers.

The Baby-sitters Club books were well-received by reviewers as well. N.R. Kleinfield, in the article "Children's Books: Inside the Baby-sitters Club," which was published in the *New York Times Book Review* in 1989, wrote that Martin's Baby-sitters Club books "are uncommonly well written for a paperback children's series."[9]

Margaret Mackey, writing in *Language Arts* in 1990 stated: "Kristy, Mary Anne, and the others seem assured of a place in the minds and hearts of at least one generation of little girls and may even be remembered fifty years from now . . ."[10]

Throughout the late 1980s and into the 1990s, the Baby-sitters Club books continued to break publishing records. In 1988 the *Los Angeles Times* book review reported that Baby-sitters Club books were outselling the number one adult books on both the fiction and nonfiction lists. "Young readers love Baby-sitters" read the front page of *USA Today* in February 1989. A few months later, nine Baby-sitters Club books were on B. Dalton's top 20 best seller list at the same time, and in December 1991 the Baby-sitters Club books

Did you know...

In 1995, a movie based on Ann M. Martin's Baby-sitters Club series called *The Baby-Sitters Club Movie* was released, with actress Schuyler Fisk playing Kristy Thomas. Martin went on location in Hollywood to help review the movie script and casting decisions. While working on the movie, Martin was surprised to learn that most of the actresses playing the characters of the baby-sitters were actually readers of her series. Martin felt, because the actresses were fans of the books, the movie captured the spirit of the Baby-Sitters Club. *The Baby-Sitters Club Movie* joined a series of videos released in the early 1990s that were also based on the Baby-Sitters Club books.

held the top three positions on *Publishers Weekly*'s best seller list. Amazingly, in 1991, 10 of the top-16 best sellers of the year were Baby-sitters Club books, each selling over 300,000 copies. By January 1996, the Baby-sitters Club books had been on *Publishers Weekly*'s best seller list consistently for over a decade, showing that there was an entire generation of pre-teen girls waiting anxiously for each new edition in the Baby-sitters Club series.

"Dear Ann," wrote one Baby-sitters Club fan, "I'm addicted . . . I've memorized almost every part of every book and still can't stop . . . Maybe there is a treatment center I can go to?"[11]

The popularity of the Baby-sitters Club books led to the development of several other related series. The Little Sisters series, the Baby-sitters Specials series, the Baby-sitters Mysteries series, the BSC Friends Forever series, the California Diaries series, and others, were all spin-offs of the original Baby-sitters Club books. In addition, the Kids in Ms. Coleman's Class series was spun off of the Little Sisters series. And because Martin often received requests for books about particular characters, a Readers Request series was created as well. With so many Baby-sitters Club books in print at the same time, Martin's books made up 35 percent of Scholastic Inc.'s trade book sales.

Most fiction writers agree that the ending of a book is the hardest to write because when a book ends, an author must let go of the characters and say good-bye. However, because Martin was writing books in a series, she was spared—at least for a time—a final parting with her characters. When she came to the end of one book, she knew she would be "meeting" them again in a future one. And so it was for almost 15 years. Then, in 2000, Martin decided to stop writing the Baby-sitters Club books and their related series.

One of Martin's reasons for making the decision had to do with the characters of the Baby-sitters Club. For the entire time the books had been in existence, the main characters had remained the same age. If they had been living in "real time," Kristy, Mary Anne, Claudia, and Stacey would have been nearly 30 years old in 2000. "The characters have been in junior high for 15 years now," Martin said. "It's time to let them move on with their lives while we're all still feeling inspired by them."[12]

Martin knew that ending the Baby-sitters Club series would be traumatic for her readers, and so to make it as easy as possible, she selected a special theme and a special title for the last Baby-sitters Club book. She called it *Graduation Day*. "I . . . knew that sharing such an important day in the lives of the BSC members with the loyal fans would be the more natural way to conclude the series," she explained.[13]

Scholastic Inc. celebrated 15 years of the Baby-sitters Club books by giving the series a farewell party in New York City. There was much to celebrate. The Baby-sitters Club series is unquestionably one of the longest running and most successful series in the history of children's publishing. From the original four Baby-sitters Club books written in 1985, the series grew to 138 books. In addition, several series had been created to offset the Baby-sitters Club series, resulting in a total of close to 400 "Baby-sitters Club" books. "It still amazes me to see the incredible body of work that was a result of that original idea," said Martin.[14]

All totaled, the Baby-sitters Club books have sold over 180 million copies in 21 countries. They have also been translated into 19 foreign languages. The Baby-sitters Club television series has aired on both HBO and the Disney Channel. A Baby-sitters Club fan club was formed in 1988 and, despite the cancellation of the series, it is still going strong. In 1995, a movie based on the Baby-sitters Club was released. Games and other merchandise centered on the Baby-sitters Club have also been produced.

According to Martin, the success of the Baby-sitters Club can be attributed to several things coming together at the right time. She feels it was a combination of having the right writers for the series, readers who were ready to read a series like the Baby-sitters Club, and a publisher such as Scholastic Inc. willing to take a chance on publishing the books. "You know, even if all these things came together now, it might not be the right time. There weren't as many series to compete with when the Baby-sitters Club first came out. It really was luck," said Martin.[15]

Although Martin was sad to see the Baby-sitters Club series end, she knew that just like Kristy, Mary Anne, Claudia, and Stacey, it was time for her to move on as well. "As much as I've loved working on the characters, it's freeing to come up with new characters and ideas," she told one interviewer.[16] In a letter written to her fans and included at the end of *Graduation Day*, Martin said that she would miss working on the books, miss spending time with the characters, and especially miss her connection to the fans of the Baby-sitters Club books. "On the other hand, I have fifteen years of memories, most of them created by you," she wrote.[17] And even though Martin would no longer be writing the Baby-sitters Club books, she would not be saying good-bye to her readers. She told her fans:

. . . [E]very time a new reader picks up a Baby-sitters Club book for the very first time, I feel as if I've found a new friend. While I am sad on one level to close this chapter of my writing life, I am also excited about the new projects that I will now have the time to explore . . . . As you probably know, what I love to do most is write books for children.[18]

Ann M. Martin has always loved reading. Growing up, her parents encouraged her to read and to be creative. In the picture above, she is reading in her home in Greenwich Village, New York, where she lived in 1989 while working on the Baby-sitters Club series.

2

"A Pretty Wonderful Childhood"

PRINCETON, NEW JERSEY, is a town of about 14,000 people. It lies on the Northeast Corridor train route between New York City and New Jersey's capital city, Trenton. To most people, the name "Princeton" is synonymous with Princeton University, the Ivy League university located in the heart of the town. Ann Matthews Martin was born in Princeton, at Princeton Hospital, on August 12, 1955. Hurricane Connie, among the most devastating of mid-summer storms to hit the northeastern part of the United States, pummeled the hospital building while Martin was being born. Because of this, Martin's father, Henry Read Martin, suggested she be named Connie Gale. Instead, her father, also called Hank, and her mother, Edith, also called Edie, chose the name Ann for their first born daughter because they liked its simplicity. For her middle name, they chose Matthews, her mother's maiden name.

Martin was born into a family that is able to trace its roots to the days of the Pilgrims. Edie's ancestors were among the 102 people that crossed the Atlantic Ocean on the Mayflower and landed at Plymouth, Massachusetts, in December 1620. They settled on land that is now part of Connecticut. Over the centuries, Edie's family found their way to Wisconsin, where Edie was raised, and then to Illinois, where she was living when she met Hank.

Hank's ancestrs were also from England. They arrived in the New World soon after the Mayflower landed, and they also settled in what is now Connecticut. The Martins eventually moved to Kentucky, where Hank was raised. In the late 1940s, Hank came east to Princeton, New Jersey, to attend Princeton University, from which he graduated in 1948. While in Princeton, he lived in the same boarding-house as Edie's parents. (They had moved from Illinois, to be closer to their son, Rick, who was a librarian at the University.) When Edie, who was working as a nursery school teacher, came to Princeton to visit, her parents introduced her to Hank. The two liked each other immediately, and were married in 1953.

Hank and Edie moved into a two-bedroom apartment in Princeton. Hank was an artist and cartoonist, whose work has appeared in the contemporary magazine, the *New Yorker*. He used the apartment's second bedroom as his studio. After they had been married for about two years, Hank and Edie learned they were expecting a baby. Hank found and rented a former tailor's shop on Charlton Street in downtown Princeton, and relocated his studio there. Then he and Edie converted his old studio back into a bedroom for the new addition to their family.

After Ann was born, Edie stayed at home to care for her. The Martins acquired their first television set around this time. From an early age, Ann enjoyed sitting on her father's lap and watching television. Her favorite television show was, and is to this day, *I Love Lucy*. (Martin now owns videos and DVDs of almost every episode of *I Love Lucy* that has ever aired.)

When Ann was 2 years old, her sister, Jane, was born. As young children, the sisters spent hours together playing with their pets, and in their play houses and tree houses. They played with their dolls in the woods near their home, creating little houses for them among the tree roots. They also enjoyed playing dress up, using old clothes stored in a second-hand trunk that Hank had painted with pictures of Winnie the Pooh. Sometimes the girls would perform plays and shows in the outfits they created.

When Ann was 4, her parents purchased three-quarters of an acre of land on a Princeton street named Dodds Lane. They built a new home on the property. Ann and her sister each had their own room. Over time more homes were constructed around the Martin's new house, and each family that moved in brought more playmates for the girls. The neighborhood was soon full of children, and winter, spring, summer, or fall, there was always something exciting happening on Dodds Lane. Ann wanted to be a part of it all. Always eager to start her day, she was a *very* early riser, so much so that her parents made a rule that she was not allowed to wake them up before 6:30 A.M.

None of Martin's grandparents lived in New Jersey, but they still were able to play a part in their grandchildren's lives. Hank's parents, Grandpoppy and Granny, lived in the

Louisville area of Kentucky. They were warm and affection-ate and they loved children. Granny taught Ann how to knit, a hobby Martin enjoys to this day. Granny lived to see Mar-tin become a successful children's-book author; she died at the age of 94 when Martin was 32. By that time, the Baby-sitters Club books had been on best seller lists for years.

Edie's parents, Neena and Grandpa, eventually left Princeton, and divided their time between Winter Park, Florida, where they lived during the winter months, and Maine, where they lived in the summer. In between, they would make visits to Princeton. While Grandpa loved to read and was always up for a game of baseball with Martin, Neena shared her love of all types of music. (She played the piano, sang in the choir, and listened to opera.) Neena also passed on her strong sense of family ties; when she and Mar-tin were together, Neena would tell countless stories about their relatives who lived long ago.

Martin and her sister Jane had a secure childhood. For the most part, they got along well, but like most siblings, they had their share of small squabbles and disagreements. Even when the girls quarreled, they did not stay mad for long.

Like opposite poles on a magnet, Martin and her sister were more dissimilar than alike. For starters, they were, and still are, very different in temperament and personality. As a child, Martin had many fears and often had nightmares. She was timid and shy. She loved books and she liked to read, or to make up stories and plays. Sometimes she just sat quietly and listened to the adults talking. Jane, on the other hand, was more boisterous and enjoyed more active pursuits. She also had a more outgoing personality. Martin enjoyed school; Jane preferred playing to studying. Martin did not like participat-ing in sports, while Jane enjoyed both soccer and lacrosse.

Jane, who eventually became a television producer,

explained the differences between her and her sister in this way:

> Ann would always come home and just be by herself. She'd do her homework and get A's. I would cut class, run to the pizza place with my friends, come in at five, watch the *Flintstones*, do a half hour of homework, and get on the phone. We were always just totally different.[19]

One of Martin's most vivid childhood memories is that of growing up surrounded by books. Edie and Hank often read to their daughters and Edie started taking the girls to the Princeton Public Library as soon as they could walk. Martin got her first library card when she was in kindergarten—as soon as she could sign her name—and her parents encouraged her to read as often as she could. As she got older, she went to the library more and more frequently. She was only allowed to borrow 10 books at a time and while she borrowed books that she had not read before most of the time, sometimes she would give in to an urge to reread one of her favorite books. Some of the books Martin particularly enjoyed as a child were *Alice in Wonderland* by Lewis Carroll, *Doctor Dolittle* by Hugh Lofting, and *The Secret Garden* by Frances Hodgson Burnett. Other childhood books that Martin took pleasure from were the *Wizard of Oz*, the books about Pippi Longstocking and her adventures, the Mrs. Piggle Wiggle books, and the mystery series of both Nancy Drew and the Bobbsey Twins.

Martin treasures the love of reading that was instilled in her as a child by her parents, and realizes it has played a large part in her wanting to be a writer. She says:

> [Reading] was a gift that was given to me as a child by many people, and now as an adult and a writer, I'm trying to give a little of it back to others. It's one of the greatest pleasures I know.[20]

Princeton University, seen here, is the heart of Princeton, New Jersey, where Ann M. Martin grew up. The Martin family moved to the developing neighborhood on Dodds Lane when Martin was four years old. Martin and her younger sister, Jane, had many friends and playmates in the close community.

Edie and Hank encouraged their daughters to be creative in several ways. Hank, as an artist, encouraged Martin and Jane to draw, paint, and work on various types of arts and crafts. Sometimes the Martin family would spend entire days together working on family projects such as making papier-mâché puppets. "It was a pretty wonderful childhood," Martin explains.[21]

From a very young age, Martin showed signs of being a storyteller, and before she was able to write, she dictated stories to her mother. When she was older, Martin would write her stories in notebooks, but she refused to share them with others. She has said:

> I grew up in a very imaginative family . . . . Both [parents] liked fantasy and children's literature, so my world was one of circuses, animals . . . elves, gnomes and fairies. It was fun and it stayed with me.[22]

The sisters often played their favorite games of Life and Clue. Love and enjoyment of games existed in the Martin household long before Martin and Jane were born. Hank Martin actually *invented* two adult games—Supermarket and Boodoggle, both of which he sold to Parker Brothers. They were produced and sold in stores, but neither is available to purchase today. Martin and her father loved to play cards, especially double solitaire. They knew and played several variations of that game. For a brief period of time, they played "thousands" of games of Hearts.[23]

Martin remembers her childhood as being "very happy years because I had parents who would read to us, take us to circuses, teach us magic tricks and toast marshmallows in the woods with us. They never cared if we made a mess. My mother called our playroom 'toy soup.'"[24]

Another of Martin's present loves that began when she was a child is her love of animals, especially cats. The Martin family kept cats as pets as she was growing up. At one time nine cats lived in the Martin home—five adult cats and four kittens. They also kept fish, guinea pigs, hamsters, mice, and turtles as pets.

One childhood memory that Martin would like to forget is the time when she was 11 years old and fell face-first out of a tree house. She had been climbing down a ladder front ways when the hem of her outfit got caught on the top of the ladder. She landed on a tree stump with the ladder crashing down on top of her. Martin's spleen—an organ that helps the body fight infections and diseases—was torn in the accident. Within a few hours, it had to be surgically removed (the surgery is called a spleenectomy) and Martin had to stay in the hospital for a week to recuperate. After the accident, she got many colds and infections during her childhood. Not having a spleen has also affected her as an adult, although she does not get sick quite as often as she did when she was a child.

Edie and Hank wanted their daughters to experience everything they could. Martin studied art, dancing, piano, and guitar. She also took horseback riding lessons, which were her favorite of all her lessons. (Her riding lessons found their way into one of her books about sibling rivalry titled *Me and Katie (the Pest)*.) She was good at whatever she tried, but when it came to sewing, she excelled. She began sewing simple projects on her mother's old Singer sewing machine when she was about 9 years old. One of the first things Martin made was a set of red, white, and blue curtains for the windows of her father's Charlton Street art studio. Not long after that, she began making clothing for some of the children in the neighborhood, as well as for herself. She saved all the money she made baby-sitting to buy a Sears Kenmore sewing machine, which she kept for 25 years.

Martin and Jane attended the Littlebrook Elementary School. Academically, Martin was a good student; she put a lot of pressure on herself to get good grades, and she succeeded. She enjoyed studying, doing homework, and working on school projects; however, socially, school was difficult for her. She was shy and uncomfortable when it was her turn to give a presentation in the front of the class. Her two worst subjects were math and social studies. Her favorite subject was English, because she liked to write. "Excellent! Excellent! Excellent!" her teacher wrote on a seventh-grade creative writing assignment.[25]

Martin was one of the older children living on Dodds Lane, but she loved playing and interacting with the younger children. According to Martin, there was always some group of younger kids to play with, organize, or take care of. Martin's best friend on Dodds Lane was Beth McKeever; Beth was slightly older than Martin and more outspoken. According to Beth, "Ann was just always there for me, and I was always there for her."[26] The fact that they had opposite personalities did not cause problems in their friendship. Beth explained:

> I was the one who would try to sew a dress and it would end up rolled up in the closet on the floor. I thought that was a fine place for it to be. Ann would stay up and make the dress work, and make it fit . . . and it would look great![27]

Martin first started taking care of children when she was 10 years old. It was then that she began working as a mother's helper for the Rice family, one of the families that lived on Dodds Lane. Martin watched three children for Mrs. Rice, giving her a chance to catch up with her chores around the house. Martin was so helpful that the Rice's took her along on their vacation to Virginia Beach.

Many of the families living on Dodds Lane managed to get away for a while during the summer. Every year Beth's family spent two weeks in Avalon, a New Jersey seaside resort. They often took Martin along on their vacations, but after a few years, the Martins rented their own beach house in Avalon, always at the same time as the McKeever family.

Martin's August birthday usually occurred during the families' vacation time, and just as if they were home, the girls were inseparable. They would ride their bikes to the beach and celebrate her birthday with a breakfast of donuts. Other favorite shore activities were playing miniature golf, walking along the small boardwalk, and, of course, spending hours on the beach. They also flirted with the lifeguards, who were much older.

The Martin family also vacationed outside of New Jersey. They traveled to Kentucky to visit Hank's family. (Grandpoppy and Granny also came to visit the Martin's in New Jersey.) Sometimes they traveled to Maine to visit with Neena and Grandpa. On another vacation, they flew to California, and then drove to Wisconsin to visit the places where Edie had lived and vacationed as a child. Another time, Martin and her family traveled to San Francisco, California. They flew first to Denver, Colorado, and then traveled the rest of the way by train. Once in California, the family visited Disneyland and other tourist attractions such as Yellowstone Park. During the long hours on the train, Martin and Jane passed the time by pretending to be one of their favorite fictional characters, Harriet, the Spy. They kept a close watch on the other passengers, then wrote their observations in a secret notebook.

The Martin family also took day trips to New York City—about an hour's train ride from Princeton. There they would see Broadway plays, the Ringling Brothers Circus, and other New York City attractions. A highlight of these trips was having a hearty lunch at Schraffts restaurant

Martin was never bored, even when she was not in school or on vacation, because she had so many interests to keep her occupied. She enjoyed art projects, swimming, and spending time with her friends. Martin loved attending sleepover parties, especially when they fell on New Year's Eve. She and her best friends would get together in their flannel nightgowns and tell each other scary stories, try out new hair styles, eat lots of food, and watch late-night television.

One summer, Martin and Jane set up a lending library in Martin's bedroom. They alphabetized their books, glued pockets on the inside back covers and placed due date cards in each pocket. All the kids on Dodds Lane were allowed to check out books, but just like a regular library, they had to return them on time, or else pay a fine of a penny a day.

Martin began baby-sitting in earnest when she was 13 and kept it up "nonstop."[28] (Even when she went to college she would baby-sit during her holiday vacations.) There was no organized Baby-sitters Club on Dodds Lane, but Martin and Beth often got together while sitting for various families. This arrangement allowed the children to play together and the baby-sitters to keep each other company while they worked. Remembering those baby-sitting days on Dodds Lane, Beth recalls that Martin was the "ultimate babysitter." She says:

> She always had something going on. She showed up with special things to do and ways to entertain the kids. She had this incredible patience about her. She genuinely loved the kids and they loved her back. There are just some things you do, and you do them well because you're so comfortable with them. Ann was that way with baby-sitting.[29]

Martin attended Princeton High School. During those high school years, the Princeton Public Library became her "home away from home" and "the perfect place to do my schoolwork, study for tests, and work on research papers and projects."[30] When she was not studying, Martin did typical teenage things. She went to dances, the movies, and to her senior prom. She volunteered as a candy striper (a teenage volunteer worker at a hospital) at Princeton Hospital and for the Red Cross Youth Group. She went to basketball and football games with her friends.

In high school, the subjects that gave her the most trouble were math and history and her favorite subjects were French and English. She says, "I was very good in school but it was always a struggle. I felt I didn't understand things—or didn't understand them fast enough. But after all that nervousness, every marking period I'd end up with great grades and good test scores."[31]

Like many students, Martin did not always like the required reading her English teachers assigned for their classes and wanted, instead, to choose her own reading material. In high school she preferred books by Ray Bradbury, Agatha Christie, and Isaac Asimov.

Martin began thinking seriously about college during her junior year of high school. She made the honor roll all four years she spent at Princeton High School, even though she overloaded herself with courses her first three years so that she could relax more easily during her senior year. One of the classes she took during her senior year was Child Care. Martin had already made the decision to study elementary education in college. She thought a course in Child Care would be good to take because it would give her the opportunity to interact with 3- and 4-year-olds.

She took the Scholastic Aptitude Test (SAT), the standard test that measures a student's readiness for college, and began investigating various colleges and universities. Once she had narrowed down her choices, she sent out a number of applications and was accepted by all the schools to which she had applied. Smith College, an all-women's college in Northampton, Massachusetts, was her first choice, and she was overjoyed when she received a letter of acceptance from them.

As her years at Princeton High School drew to a close, Martin knew the decision to become a teacher was the right one for her, because she still loved being around children. It seemed that they loved being with her, trusting and looking up to her, and because of this, she knew she could have a positive impact on their lives. And so, on a warm June evening in 1973, she put on a cap and gown and, along with the rest of her senior class, received her high school diploma. Martin graduated Princeton High School with high honors. The following September she started college and began working towards her towards her goal of becoming an elementary school teacher.

Did you know...

Ann M. Martin's alma mater is Smith College, an all-women's college in Northampton, Massachusetts. Smith College was founded in 1871 and continues to be the largest liberal arts college for women in the United States.

Not surprisingly, Smith College has graduated many students who, like Martin, have gone on to become successful authors. Smith College's author roster includes well-known children's book authors such as Madeleine L'Engle who wrote the 1963 Newbery Medal winner *A Wrinkle in Time* and Jane Yolen, author of *The Devil's Arithmetic*. It also includes such well-known authors of adult literature as Margaret Mitchell, who wrote *Gone with the Wind*; Sylvia Plath, author of *The Bell Jar*; and Betty Friedan, author of *The Feminine Mystique*.

Because of her love for children, Ann M. Martin decided to go to college to become an elementary school teacher for special needs children. Martin attended Smith College in Northampton, Massachusetts, shown here, and double-majored in elementary education and child psychology.

3

From Editor to Writer

SOCIAL RESPONSIBILITY and volunteerism (the act of doing volunteer work in community service) have always been important values in the Martin family. Neena, Edie's mother, instilled the importance of volunteerism in her daughter, and Edie, in turn, passed it down to her own children. Martin's parents taught their daughters by word and example that everyone can make a difference in the world—every little word or action counts.

The Martin family contributed money and sent letters to an overseas child welfare organization. Later, as a teenager, one of

Martin's volunteer jobs was with the Red Cross Youth Group. One way she helped the organization raise money was by holding various fundraisers, such as cake sales. Her work with the Red Cross Youth Group led to another volunteer job: working at a summer day camp for developmentally-disabled children. Here Martin was able to use the skills that had caused Beth McKeever to call her "the ultimate babysitter." She played games with the children, did arts and crafts, and went on walks with them. It was clear to all that Martin had a natural talent for interacting with children with special needs. She enjoyed working with these special children so much that she also took a summer job at the Eden Institute, a nearby school for children with autism.

Autism is not a disease. It is a brain disorder usually first diagnosed in childhood. Autistic children have difficulty communicating and interacting with others, both verbally and nonverbally. They may have difficulty speaking. They sometimes repeat the same action—for example, rocking back and forth—over and over again. Autism is a life-long condition, however many people with this disorder are able to go on to live independently or partially assisted as adults. At the present time there is no known single cause of autism, nor is there a cure.

Martin's work with autistic children has given her a special way of looking at the disorder. She says, "These children are probably born with complete use of normal mental faculties, but they're so locked inside themselves that they have no way to communicate. I sometimes wonder . . . what it must feel like to be bright and have no way to communicate."[32]

Martin worked all four of her high school summers at the Eden Institute. By her third summer, she was allowed to

Ann M. Martin spent her summers as a teenager working at
the Eden Institute in Princeton, New Jersey, shown above, where
she helped autistic children and adolescents improve their learning
and communication skills. Martin has always loved working with
children and the summers she spent at the Eden Institute changed
her life forever.

work with a few children on a one-on-one basis. She set up specific goals and challenges for each child. Often one of her charges would forget skills that had been previously learned. Then Martin would help the child review what had been forgotten.

Sometimes she would take her students to the Princeton Pool, where other pool-goers would stare at their odd behaviors. David Holmes, the Director of the Eden Institute, praised Martin for helping her students to live as normally as possible. "As a member of the Princeton community, [Martin] showed the rest of the people of the town that she cared about these kids and that she thought they had a right to be in the pool and in the community. She was making a real statement . . ." he said.[33]

When she went to Smith College, Martin declared herself as a "double major"—she chose to major in both elementary education and child psychology. She felt the combination of these two courses of study would give her a good foundation for becoming a teacher, especially a teacher of children with special needs. While attending Smith College, she lived with 60 other women in a college residence called Gardner House. She became friends with many of the girls who lived on her floor, most of whom were upperclassmen. In these new friends Martin found companionship, which served her well when college life got tough, providing shoulders to lean on.

Martin took her college courses as seriously as she had her high school courses. For the most part, her housemates were as studious as she, and most evenings the group of women could be found studying in the library. The girls rarely watched television, so to de-stress after a study session they would eat and talk, and tell one another about their families. One of Martin's friends, Kate Durbin has said of the group: "We were all good listeners. It was a very tight circle in terms of emotional support. But we all shared the same silly sense of humor. We had a lot of fun."[34]

When Martin did have a little down time, she tutored patients at a nearby state mental institute and taught sewing in an after-school program. She also wrote for Smith College's newspaper, *The Sophian*. Sometimes she would visit nearby Yale University with the girls from Gardner House, but she rarely did so. The grueling courses she signed up for required much studying, which left little time for socializing.

One of the requirements to become a teacher was to spend a set number of hours "practice teaching." Martin was fortunate in that she was able to do her practice teaching right on campus at the Smith College Campus School. Martin was assigned lower grades—kindergarten one semester and first grade the second. She found both classes enjoyable to work with.

It was while she was at Smith College that Martin became reacquainted with the writings she had loved as a child. To meet one of her elementary education requirements, Martin took a course in children's literature. Not only did she read books written for children, she studied them and took notes on their authors, their illustrations, and how best they could be used to help children. For example, Martin would note whether a particular book taught a lesson or emphasized a concept. Was it written purely for entertainment, or did it have an educational value? How could the book best be used in the classroom? Martin kept all of her notes in a file. When she was a senior, she had to write a thesis for each of her majors. For her elementary education major, Martin wrote a 50-page paper on the use of children's literature in the classroom.

Martin's renewed interest in children's literature reawakened her desire to write, especially books for children. While she was at Smith College, she quietly began submitting a few picture book manuscripts to publishers, but they were all rejected.

In 1977, Martin graduated with honors from Smith College. She had a job lined up; she was going to be a teacher at Plumfield School in Noroton, Connecticut. This was a school for special elementary school-aged children—those with dyslexia (a condition where the brain is unable to translate images received from the eyes or ears into an understandable language) or other conditions—who needed help in some way. Her experience working with children with special needs as a summer camp counselor, as well as at the

Did you know...

Ann M. Martin took only one creative writing class while she was at Smith College. Martin says it is her "on-the-job" experience in both teaching and publishing that has given her a solid background for writing for children. She explains that she learned about children by working with them as a teacher, and she learned about writing from reading other people's manuscripts as an editor. Martin gives "equal weight" to both activities when it comes to furthering her career as a writer.

Eden Institute, had shown Martin that she had a gift of working with special children. At Plumfield School, she
co-taught fourth and fifth graders. She rented an apartment
near the school, and visited her family in New Jersey on
weekends.

Although she was a gifted teacher, Martin left Plumfield
School after one year. Soon after, she left teaching alto-
gether. Her love of reading and of children's books was taking her in a completely new direction. Martin realized she
would like to work in the children's book publishing industry. She took a position with the New York-based publisher
Pocket Books, as an editorial assistant for one of its
imprints, Archway Paperbacks. Martin found she enjoyed
this unexpected detour in her career path, and every aspect
of the creative side of the children's publishing business fascinated her.

Two other positions in the children's publishing industry
followed. In 1980, Martin became a copywriter—a writer
of publicity material—at Scholastic Inc. in the Teen Age
Book Club department. While at Scholastic Inc., she was
promoted to associate editor, and then worked her way up
to editor. She stayed at Scholastic Inc. until 1983, when she
became senior editor for Bantam's Books for Young Readers.

Every day that she worked in the publishing field, Martin
was surrounded by manuscripts for children's books. It
became increasingly difficult to be in the midst of creating
books for young readers and not be writing one of her own.
Martin had an idea for a book which she had been toying
with for a while. When she was 25 years old, she began writing *Bummer Summer*, the story of 12-year-old Kammy
Whitlock, whose widowed father remarries a younger

woman with two children. Kammy fights the adjustments she has to make, accepting the presence of a stepmother and step-siblings in her life. Believing her father and stepmother are just trying to get rid of her, she agrees to give summer camp a two-week try. While there, Kammy learns to accept her father's marriage and her new family; she also discovers a few things about herself.

It took Martin over a year to write *Bummer Summer* because she was still working full time in publishing, and could only write before work in the mornings, and on weekends. Friendships and connections are important. When the manuscript was finished, Martin showed it to a friend who knew someone who knew Amy Berkower, an agent who represents authors of children's books. Amy sent *Bummer Summer* to three publishing houses. One of them, Holiday House, liked the manuscript, but asked Martin to make revisions. It took another year and a half to rewrite the manuscript so that it was acceptable to Holiday House, but finally, *Bummer Summer* was published in 1983.

*R*eviewers and young readers had differing opinions about *Bummer Summer*. One reviewer, writing in *School Library Journal* wrote "this first novel falters in trying to handle two themes (stepfamily, first time at camp) at once. Both issues receive little more than a quick gloss.[35]

Another reviewer was more positive, saying "[*Bummer Summer*] is capably written for a first novel, has adequate pace, characters that are believable . . . and a patterned plot."[36]

Young readers, however, reacted favorably to the novel, and named *Bummer Summer* to the Children's Choice List, a survey of children's books administered by a joint committee of the Children's Book Council and the International Reading Association.

Martin had no way of knowing at the time that *Bummer Summer* would be the first of hundreds of books she would write. *Bummer Summer* not only changed her life, but because it established Martin as a writer, it changed the face of children's publishing as well.

Besides Ann M. Martin's vivid imagination, children have always been an inspiration for her books. Martin enjoys spending time with her young fans, reading and interacting with students who love to read. Above, Martin is surrounded by fans of her official fan club at the Public School 2 in New York City's Chinatown.

4

Going Freelance

AFTER *BUMMER SUMMER* was published, Martin continued to work as a senior editor at Bantam Books for Young Readers. She also continued to write her middle-grade-fiction books. Martin's habit of rising early stayed with her into adulthood, and she continued to write in the mornings before heading off to work. By 1986, she had four more books to her credit: *Inside Out*, a story based upon her work with autistic children at Eden Institute; *Stage Fright*, the story of a 9-year-old girl, who, like Martin, is very shy; *Me and Katie (the Pest)*, a story of sibling rivalry loosely based on Martin's childhood with her sister, Jane;

and *With You and Without You*, the story of a young girl coping with the death of her father.

All five of Martin's books were well-received by young readers. She had proven to herself, and others, that she could write books that young people wanted to read. In 1985, Martin decided she was ready to leave her position as an editor and dedicate herself to writing from her home. It was a big step to take, and one that required preparation and planning. Martin would be saying good-bye to a job that provided her with a steady income, a pension, and other benefits, to start a career that depended solely on her ability to produce books that young people wanted to read and buy. She had saved up some money to tide her over, but before she could make her leave from Bantam official, Martin had to be sure she could generate enough income to support herself. Therefore, in addition to writing, Martin decided she would also take on freelance editing work.

Martin's friend, Kate Durbin, has said, "In a lot of ways [Martin] would strike people as timid and not able to take the kind of risk that would allow her to quit her job . . . . There's a great deal of strength inside her."[37]

Martin had met many people and had made many contacts while working in the publishing field; now she informed everyone she knew that she was going out on her own and that she was looking for writing and editing opportunities. Fortunately, Martin had made a name for herself in publishing. Not only was she known for her excellent writing, but also for being a dependable and reliable person. Word got around, and Martin's contacts provided her with enough freelance writing and editing work to keep her going during those first few months of professional independence.

Freelancers—in any profession—work for themselves. Perhaps it could be said that freelancing runs in the Martin

"Excuse me, may I see your invitation?"

Creativity seems to run in the Martin family. Ann M. Martin's father, Henry Martin, was an artist and illustrator who often had cartoons in The New Yorker *magazine. Above is one of his illustrations from the magazine, depicting a confused tea party in Alice's Wonderland.

family. For many years, Martin's father, Hank, worked as a freelance cartoonist and artist. In a sense, he was a role model for Martin. His working habits gave Martin a good idea of what the freelance life was like. It is easy to let yourself waste time watching television or talking to friends on the phone when there is no boss looking over your shoulder, watching over you. It does not matter what field you work in, when you are a freelancer, *you* are your own boss, and it is up to you to demonstrate the self-discipline needed to get your work done.

Hank was a dedicated professional. Day after day he went to his office on Charlton Street and put in a full eight hours of work. Martin saw that her hard-working father had to maintain a strict work schedule in order to be productive and she found that she has the same work ethic as her father. Over the 20 years that she has been a freelance writer, Martin has developed a writing system that works well for her. She writes Tuesdays through Fridays, and she takes Mondays off to relax. Often she will use her day off to sew or work on her other hobbies.

On her writing days, Martin rises early, and gets her chores done and out of the way. She is usually at her desk by 9:00 A.M. at the latest. First she checks her e-mail and then she gets ready to write. (She does her best writing in the morning because that is when she is freshest.) Martin has intense powers of concentration. Once she begins her work for the day, she is able to block out all outside interferences or distractions. Her cats are her only companions when she writes. Martin can write anywhere, but she must have absolute silence to work—no talking, television, or music.

The first thing that Martin does when she begins her writing day is to read over and revise the material that she wrote the day before. She does this before writing anything new. When she first began writing books, Martin wrote all of her manuscripts at her dining room table in long hand on yellow lined tablets. She then gave the hand-written pages to an assistant, who typed them up for editing. A few years ago, however, Martin learned to use a computer and now she types her manuscripts directly into the computer; she still edits on paper.

One important technique that Martin finds helpful when writing books is outlining. To Martin, an outline of a book is like a map: it gets her where she is going. Martin's outlines have, at times, resembled miniature books. They are very detailed and can fill 20 or more pages. Even if something in the story changes as Martin is writing, she still finds it helpful to have an outline to guide her. She finds that when she runs into "writer's block" (a term writers use for not being able to think of what to write next), having an outline from which to work keeps her focused. "If I get stuck—which does happen—I try to force myself to write. If I'm really stuck, I put it away and go back to it the next day. I never stop at the end of a chapter—it's always easier for me to begin in the middle of something," she said.[38] Martin says that if she runs into writer's block, she just leaves off in the middle of a sentence. When she resumes her work, just finishing that one sentence is all she needs to get going again.

In the afternoons, Martin reads, edits her work, attends meetings, and answers her fan mail. She reads newspapers, magazines, and recently published books to help her come up with writing ideas, and also to help her keep up with what's new in the areas she writes about. Sometimes the ideas for new books come from personal experiences or the experiences of those she is close to. Martin has a good memory and she will often reach back into her own childhood and use things that actually happened to her, or members of her family, as a foundation upon which to build a story or part of a story. She explains:

> One of the most important tools I use in my writing is my memory. It is very clear. I can remember what that first day of kindergarten was like—the way the room looked, the children, how I felt when my mother left. And I remember my senior prom and my tenth birthday and vacations at the shore and junior high graduation just as clearly. Little things, too—making a bulletin board display in sixth grade and making doll clothes and playing statute after dinner on hot summer nights. It's just as important to be able to transport oneself back to childhood as it is to have a vivid imagination, in order to write believable children's books.[39]

Observing children and reading their fan mail also gives Martin ideas for stories. The characters in her books are all fictitious, but they are based upon real people. She gives her characters names she likes, or the names of people she knows. (For example, Martin had a housemate in Gardner House named Claudia). Sometimes she names the pets in her stories after real pets she has had or known. (Martin had a cat named Mouse who has shown up in her books and Beth McKeever Perkins's family dog, Chewbacca, has also been part of the Baby-sitter Club books.)

Martin keeps ideas in the back of her mind, so that as soon as she has finished writing one book, she can immediately begin another. Deadlines are something all freelancers must deal with. Keeping such a strict writing schedule has helped Martin miss very few of them. She likes to work on more than one book at a time and feels she writes her best when she is juggling many different projects. Martin says that the very beginning of a story is often just an idea—sometimes a single sentence—that comes to her. She will spend a few weeks thinking about the idea until she is ready to outline it. Once it has been outlined, Martin feels the story is truly on its way to being written.

Most of Martin's books are written from a young girl's point of view. This is because writing in a girl's voice comes naturally to her. However, Martin believes that just because her books are written from a girl's point of view, does not mean that boys cannot enjoy them, also. Occasionally Martin does write in a boy's voice. Her book, *Inside Out*, was written from the point of view of an 11-year-old boy named Jonno whose brother, James, is autistic. *Ma and Pa Dracula*, a fantasy about a boy who was adopted by vampires, was written in the voice of a fourth-grade boy, Jonathan Primave.

Another technique Martin makes use of in her writing is

dialogue. There is a lot of conversation in Martin's books, as she prefers to fill her pages with dialogue in place of straight descriptive text. She uses dialogue as a way of letting her readers know which way a plot is unfolding, and what is happening with the characters. In order to get her dialogue just right, Martin listens to conversations, especially those of young people who are around the same age as the characters in her books. Her vivid memory also allows her to remember conversations she had with friends when she was young. Martin uses some of what she hears and remembers when writing dialogue for her characters.

Martin finds plotting the most difficult part of writing a story, but she enjoys becoming her characters for a brief time. Because her books are so heavily outlined, Martin can

Did you know...

Ann M. Martin has written several books under the name Ann Matthews, with titles such as *Punky Brewster and the Great Dog Escape* and *Punky Brewster and the Nothing-to-do Day*. These books are based on the 1984 television hit series, *Punky Brewster*, which is about a girl named Penelope "Punky" Brewster, whose mother abandons her and her dog, Brandon, while they are shopping. Punky befriends photographer Henry Warnimont who is the manager of their apartment building. Throughout the series, which ended in 1988, Henry looks out for Punky and in return Punky's youthful joy changes Henry's life. The books are targeted to readers ages 4–8, and were published by Wanderer Books in 1986.

tell when it is time to end a book. "Even so, it's sometimes hard to write the very last sentence. It's the last thing the reader will read and it has to be just right," she says.[40]

When she started freelance writing in 1985, Martin never intended to write a series of books that would be so popular with young readers. "All I really wanted was to publish two hard covers a year and help support myself writing catalog copy, jacket blurbs, *anything* to make ends meet," she said.[41]

When she was asked to write the Baby-sitters Club books, it was unquestionably the most exciting assignment she had received since she began freelance writing. At the time Jean Feiwel proposed the idea to Martin, the concept of a series written exclusively about a group of girls was a relatively new one. Series books in general were popular; the sales of Nancy Drew books, Trixie Beldon books, Lucy Maud Montgomery's Anne of Green Gables series, and Laura Ingalls Wilder's Little House on the Prairie books had drawn many readers. Although the settings for these books did not take place in the 1980s, their sales demonstrated that young people enjoyed reading about the same characters in different situations. In 1984, Bantam Books released its Sweet Valley High series about girls who lived in the fictional Southern California town of Sweet Valley. The popularity of these books signaled to publishers that there were many young readers who were interested in reading about modern girls and the situations they found themselves in.

It took more than Martin's writing to create the Baby-sitters Club series, and producing each book was the result of the coordination of time and energy of several people. Because there were so many day-to-day tasks that needed to be done in order for the Baby-sitters Club books to be successful, Martin had the opportunity to work with many people, several of whom became close friends. Besides Jean

Feiwel, Martin worked with editors Bethany Buck, David Levithan, and Kate Egan.

When a new Baby-sitters Club book was being planned for the series, Martin would first meet with Jean and Bethany, and together, as a team, they would decide which direction the book would take. The three always met at least once a year to map out the course of the books for the next twelve months, and to design a style of writing for the series.

"There's a difference between writing for boys, versus girls—in 'The Hardy boys,' it's action-driven, there's event after event, situation after situation. Baby Sitters' books are character-driven. When we sit down to develop and plot or plan these books, we don't say, 'What going to happen?' but 'Who is this book about?' A Claudia plot doesn't translate to Stacey." Jean explained.[42]

After her editorial meeting with Jean and Bethany, Martin would put together a long outline detailing the book's plot, the characters to be involved, and where the action would occur. Each Baby-sitters Club book was formulaic, written to center around one of the babysitters, containing one baby-sitting conflict and one personal conflict in 15 chapters, and measuring 150 to 175 pages in length. After Martin was finished writing the outline, she and Bethany would review it. Bethany suggested changes as she saw fit and then Martin would write the book from the edited and agreed-upon outline.

Several series were "spun off" from the original Baby-sitters Club series. The first two were published in 1988. In July of that year, the first Baby-sitters Club Super Special book, *Baby-sitters on Board!* was published, and in August, the first book in the Little Sisters series, *Karen's Witch* was released. The Little Sisters series was based on the fictional Kristy Thomas's younger sister, Karen. Jean Feiwel explained how this series came about:

> The Little Sister series evolved because Martin was completely smitten with Karen. Karen was always a shining light in the Baby-sitters Club series. She came to life fully formed and talking too loudly. She was just very strong. When you develop lesser characters, sometimes they stay in the background for a few books until they come into their own. Karen was somebody who just leapt out. From the very beginning, Ann had a very clear picture of exactly who she was.[43]

Martin agrees with Jean's reasoning and calls Karen her alter-ego. She has said many times that Karen is who she wishes she could be.

The Little Sisters books were written for readers ages 7 to 10, younger than those reading the Baby-sitters Club books. Their plots centered on events that would be more important to younger children rather than the Baby-sitters Club's pre-teen audience. And unlike the Baby-sitters Club books where each story is told by a different character, all of the books in the Little Sisters series were narrated by Karen. Although for this series Martin wrote in a younger and more playful voice, she never talked down to her readers. In fact she often used words a little above the targeted age range's reading level. According to Martin, she was not

> consciously saying to myself, all right, there are seven-year-olds who are going to be reading this book; I can't use this word. I don't do that. In fact, I like to make kids stretch a little when they're reading my books. I've gotten letters from kids who have said, 'I really love your books, but I had to look up this word and that word to understand it. But they did it, and that's what I like.[44]

In June 1992, the first Baby-sitters Club Special Edition Readers' Request Book was published. Martin explained on the Scholastic Inc. website how this series came about: "You might be surprised to know how much letters from fans can influence an author. For example, I got so much mail asking for a special story for Shannon and for Logan that I decided that they should each get their own Readers' Request book."[45] The books that resulted were *Logan's Story*, *Logan Bruno, Boy Baby-Sitter*, and *Shannon's Story*.

In November 1994, the first Baby-sitters Club Portrait Collection, *Stacey's Book*, was released. Using an autobiographical format, The Portrait Collection allowed each babysitter to complete a Stoneybrook Middle School assignment by telling her life story. In September 1995, a new series, The Kids in Ms. Colman's Class debuted. This was a spin-off of the Little Sisters books and detailed the adventures of Karen's second grade class at Stoneybrook Academy.

Another series that developed from the Baby-sitters books was the California Diaries series, which was released in the Fall of 1997. In these books, Dawn, one of the Baby-sitters Club members moves to California. The books are written for readers in the 11- to 14-year-old age range. Martin explains the series by saying:

> I had been hearing for years from readers who had outgrown the Baby-sitters club and wished there was something else they could move on to that would let them stay in touch with these same characters. The only way we could envision doing this was to create another series that would involve at least one of the 13-year-old baby-sitters interacting with older kids.[46]

When Dawn moves to California, the private school that she is enrolled in is so overcrowded that the eighth-graders have to attend classes in the high school. This scenario, according to Martin, "thrust [the characters in the book] into a more sophisticated crowd of kids, and they become involved in situations a bit edgier than any found in the Baby-sitters Club stories."[47]

Martin found the diary format of this series challenging. "You have to consider realistically how long any kid would keep up a diary entry, and you must make things happen within short spaces . . . . it is compelling for kids to imagine they're sharing someone's diary—it somehow makes the reading much more intimate," she said.[48]

Other Baby-sitters Club "spin off" series were: the Mystery series, the Super Mysteries series, and the Best Friends Forever series. Once the demand for Baby-sitters Club books and the other series escalated, Martin was usually writing two books a month: one Baby-sitter Club book, and one Little Sister book. Sometimes she would work on two or three books simultaneously. In order to write this many books, Martin had to keep to a strict schedule of writing a certain number of pages per day.

As the books in the various series multiplied, almost 40 Baby-sitters Club books or spin-off series books were being produced annually. When the writing became too overwhelming for one person, Martin started outlining each story and handing the outline over to a specially chosen, small group of "ghost writers" who were familiar with the characters. Martin would then edit their writing. From the very first Baby-sitters book, Martin had instilled the characters in her stories with the values of friendship, honesty, reliability, loyalty, and a dedication to hard work. Her commitment to her readers made her want to ensure that all the books that bore her name reflected these same principles and standards.

While the best seller lists prove that young readers enjoy books written in a series format, the merits of this type of children's literature is often the subject of debate among educators and librarians. There are those who feel that series books stunt readers because they are constantly reading about the same characters.

Martin has another way of looking at books produced in a series. She has acknowledged that the Baby-sitters Club books "aren't great literature,"[49] however, she knows they are of value. She believes books produced in a series give a child who normally does not like to read the opportunity to really get to know a series' characters and to become familiar and comfortable with them. Martin is also aware that the Baby-sitters Club books attract reluctant readers and readers with learning disabilities, such as dyslexia.

While Martin advocates reading books in a series, she also knows young readers need to read a variety of reading material, and therefore, she would like to see readers of her series read other literature as well. At the same time, she hopes that reluctant readers who become interested in the Baby-sitters Club series will enjoy the experience of reading itself and from there "graduate" to other kinds of books.

When Martin ended the Baby-sitters Club series and all of its spin offs after almost 15 years, she did so with one final book, *Graduation Day*. In the back of the book, Martin included a letter thanking her readers for the success of the series. She wrote:

> The series wouldn't have lasted so long without the support of many people, but especially without you—the loyal BSC readers. Over the years, I've felt a great connection to my readers. I've received thousands of amazing letters—letters with suggestions for plots, letters of thanks, and letters from kids who simply wanted to share their lives with me. I've met readers at book signings, at schools and through contests. Of all the wonderful things that have happened to me as a result of the Babysitters Club, getting to know my readers was one of the best.[50]

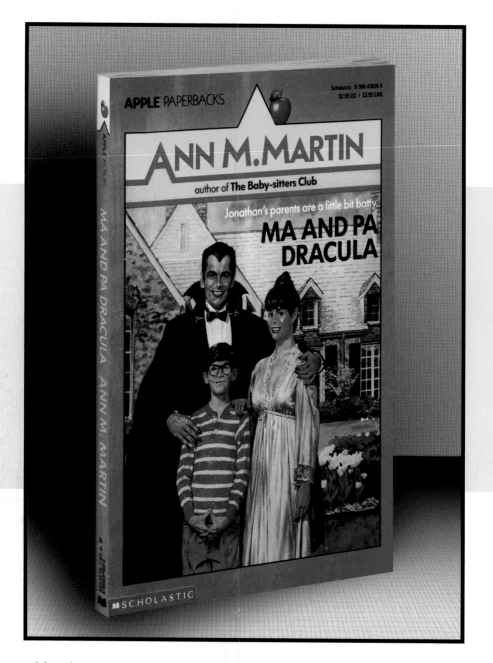

Although Ann M. Martin gained immediate fame for the Baby-sitters Club series, she has written other popular books, from light-hearted preteen books like Ma and Pa Dracula, *shown above, to books addressing more serious topics for young adults.*

5

Writing Beyond
the Series

WHILE THE MAJORITY of book reviewers gave favorable reviews to the Baby-sitter Club series, others were critical of the series and its writer. One reviewer wrote:

> I dozed off while reading one [book] outside on a nice day. A playful wind riffled through the pages so that when I woke up I'd missed 3 chapters. And I didn't notice. But children do . . . They don't seemed bothered by the lack of weighty themes.[51]

Another reviewer found the plots of the books in the Baby-sitters Club series predictable, and the language simple. Still another questioned whether quickly-written books offered enough intellectual content and good writing. "At what point does mass marketing turn books into just another set of toys?" Susan Ferraro, asked in the *New York Times* article entitled "Girl Talk."[52]

Martin's writing endured other criticisms as well. Parents complained that their children were too interested in the Baby-sitter's Club books and that they continued to read them long after their reading levels had improved beyond the series' targeted fourth grade reading level. Professionals believed the Baby-sitters Club series stereotyped girls and modeled child care and domesticity to them, instead of challenging them to explore nontraditional careers. Other critiques said that the Baby-sitters Club books limited their readers' expectations of preadolescent experiences. Martin's young readers, however, disagreed. "The books describe life as it really is for girls of that age," said one 10-year-old reader.[53]

Jean Feiwel added, "So many of the fans' letters say 'These books are about me,' 'Stacey is me,' 'Claudia is me.'"[54]

Whether reviewers liked or disliked the Baby-sitters club series was irrelevant to the young girls who were reading Martin's books. If skyrocketing book sales were any indication, Martin's readers continued to love and appreciate her books. Although she was more than twice their ages, Martin's realistic writing helped her forge a connection to her readers. She was able to do this because she relied on her powerful memory, and was able to reach back through the years and remember how if felt to be her readers' ages. All who know Martin know how important it is for her as a writer to be true to her story. "There's a lot of Martin in her books," said Beth McKeever Perkins. "She really cares about the words she writes and who she writes them for. She listens to kids and understands their sensitivity, like how it feels to wear the wrong-colored sneakers or be snubbed in the lunch line."[55]

Martin wrote the Baby-sitters Club books for the enjoyment of her readers, yet she was able to use them to tackle tough subjects such as divorce, death, and illnesses like juvenile diabetes. Martin received the most letters from readers about the books that addressed these sorts of tough issues. It appeared that the readers could connect most easily with those books.

Martin had standards when it came to what she would write about. Although each Baby-sitters Club book dealt with a specific challenge, Martin deliberately avoided the topics of sex, drugs, and child abuse in the series because she was aware that children as young as 6 years old were reading them. To Martin, these topics and others like them were too "heavy" for younger readers. That did not mean that Martin did not address topics that should have been covered. Martin concentrated on having the girls in the Baby-sitters Club focus on what she knew to be the day-to-day issues that young girls deal with: relationships with friends, parents, and teachers; getting good grades; interacting with boys; and self esteem. Susan Ferraro explains it this way in "Girl Talk": "Family stress abounds in Stoneybrook: between them, the girls cope with split marriages, the deaths of a mother and grandmother, parents who date, bicoastal families or blended households with step siblings."[56]

Martin also listened to her readers and wrote books that covered the topics they wished to read about. One theme that was constantly requested was a story that dealt with the death of a friend and how readers could cope with this tragedy. Martin responded by writing *Mary Anne and the Memory Garden*, about a young girl who is killed by a drunk driver. After the book was published, Martin received many touching letters from readers telling her that the book had helped them deal with personal losses in their own lives.

When Scholastic Inc. decided to end the Baby-sitters Club series, Martin said that it felt like a great luxury to be able to devote all of her time to writing books that were not part of the series. While writing the Baby-sitters Club series, Martin had been careful not to tackle topics that were too "heavy." Now she was free to step outside the confines of the series and write about other issues she cared about and felt were important to explore. Martin had proven she was capable of writing about heavier issues with her early books including *Inside Out* and *With You and Without You*, both of which addressed sensitive subjects. Martin's fans welcomed the chance to read about these weightier issues. When *Inside Out* was released, Martin got many letters from readers who lived with a handicapped brother or sister, who wrote to tell her it how it affected their families and their friendships.

One thing Martin keeps in mind as she writes her books is who her readers are and the messages they will take away from her books. She knows how vulnerable children are and how they are affected by the things they read, or hear, or see. At the same time, Martin wants her books to realistically portray subjects that young people want to read about. "I'm not in love with books that are full of four-letter words, but I think some kids have a need to read about certain sensitive subjects. I can only hope that such subjects are handled [by those who write about them] with foresight and knowledge of kids today. Writers need to keep their audience in mind," Martin told an interviewer for Contemporary Authors Online.[57]

Throughout the late 1980s, as she was writing the Baby-sitters Club books, Martin was simultaneously writing her own middle-grade-fiction novels. In 1986, she released *Missing Since Monday*. This book was written for a slightly older reading group and sensitively dealt with the subject of kidnapping. High school-age siblings, Maggie and Mike Ellis are put in charge of their 4-year-old stepsister, Courtenay, while their father and his new wife—Courtenay's mother—are on their honeymoon. When Courtenay does not arrive home on the school bus one day, Maggie and Mike realize she has been kidnapped. Martin balanced the serious nature of this book's plot with practical information a young person could use to avoid being kidnapped.

In *Slam Book*, Martin tackles the subject of friendship gone awry and the damage revealing your "true feelings" towards someone can do. The book illustrates the need to be responsible for our actions and also gets into other "tough" subjects like divorce and sex. This book was not as well liked as some of Martin's other books and although the plot is a dramatic one, some readers and reviewers found the characters in *Slam Book* to be more shallow than in Martin's other books.

Martin tackled dyslexia in *Yours Turly, Shirley*, which was published in 1988. This was an important subject for Martin to write about because her sister, Jane had been diagnosed with dyslexia when she was younger. Martin was also able to apply her experience working with dyslexic children at Plumfield School to this book.

In the late 1990s, Martin tackled the subject of the desegregation of schools in *Belle Teal*, Martin's first post-Babysitters Club book. *Belle Teal* began as a short story which Martin wrote as a contribution to a book entitled, *Smith Voices—Selected Works by Smith College Alumni*, edited by one of her former Smith College English professors. Martin continued to be fascinated by this character after the short

Segregation and civil rights were hot topics when Ann M. Martin was growing up, but she decided against writing about the controversial issues for many years. In her book published in 2004, Here Today, *Martin set the story in the year 1963, the year President Kennedy was shot and segregation protesters congregated at the Washington Monument, pictured above.*

story had been published, and decided to expand Belle's story into a book.

Belle Teal is a 10-year-old girl, living in rural America in the early 1960s at the time school desegregation was taking place. Martin was interested in writing about the topic of desegregation because it had occurred when she was a child. Prior to May 17, 1954, the date the Supreme Court decided "Brown vs. the Board of Education of Topeka, Kansas," public schools were segregated—black children and white children were educated in separate schools. The Supreme Court's landmark decision stated that racial separation in United States public schools was unconstitutional. As a result, every public school had to desegregate, or open its doors to all students, regardless of race.

"Although I was aware that desegregation was taking place when I was Belle Teal's age, I had not witnessed it firsthand," Martin told Linda M. Castellitto of Book-sense.com.[58] Martin does remember, however, when the first African-American student joined her class, and her teacher's explanation of desegregation.

Martin did research on the history of American school desegregation so that she would be able to tell Belle Teal's story of this "historic Civil Rights event" accurately. To provide realistic background material for the book, Martin studied the events that occurred in Little Rock, Arkansas, in 1957 when nine African-American students desegregated Central High School.

The Little Rock School Board had created a plan that would gradually integrate its schools, beginning at the high-school level, in September 1957. However, when the African-American students attempted to enter Central High as planned on September 4, 1957, they were met by angry crowds and turned away by the Arkansas National Guard, which had been called out by Arkansas Governor Orval Faubus to keep peace. Later that month, the governor was ordered to remove the National Guard. Three days later, amidst crowds protesting in front of the school, the nine students were slipped into the school through a side door. When the crowd became restless, the students were secretly removed from the school. Eventually 1,000 members of the 101st Airborne Division were sent by President Dwight Eisenhower to Little Rock. Escorted by the U.S. Army, the nine students entered the front doors of Central High School and officially began their education at the school on September 25, 1957.

To further help her with her research, Martin also read about Ruby Bridges, who, in November 1960, became one of the first African-American children to desegregate elementary schools in New Orleans, Louisiana. Ruby had been one of six black children chosen to integrate the school system, and she was the only black student who attended William Frantz Public School that year. For her own protection, Ruby had to be escorted to and from school by Federal Marshals. Elements of both the Central High School and the William Frantz Public School integration can be found in the pages of *Belle Teal*. Both *Publishers Weekly* and *Child* magazine named *Belle Teal* the best book of 2001. It was also named a BookSense.com "Children's Pick" for the same year.

One of Martin's most poignant novels is *Here Today*, which was published in 2004. *Here Today* is written in many layers, with many sub plots and sub themes comprising the book's several conflicts. Martin sets *Here Today* in 1963 and uses the assassination of President Kennedy to set the time frame of the book. Like many other Martin novels, this story is told from the point of view of a young girl, and addresses a sensitive topic—a mother's abandonment. *Here Today* is Martin's third novel set in the 1960s. "I grew up during this time and I was eight years old when President Kennedy was killed. Because my memories of that day are still very vivid, I've always wanted to incorporate that unique time in our history into one of my stories," she posted on the Scholastic Books website.[59]

Martin is a well-rounded author whose writing also reflects humor. In 1988, she wrote *Ten Kids, No Pets*, the idea for which came from her interest in big families and her love of animals. Martin thought the combination of a big family and the idea of wanting to have a pet would make a good story. *Ten Kids, No Pets*, written for readers ages 9 through 12 introduces Martin's readers to the Rosso family, which includes 10 children. The Rossos move from New York City to the country. Martin structured the plot of this book by dedicating one chapter to each of the 10 Rosso siblings, all of whom desperately beg their parents for a pet. *Ten Kids, No Pets* was selected as a Pacific Northwest Library Association award winner in 1991. Martin followed up *Ten Kids, No Pets* with a sequel, *Eleven Kids, One Summer*, in which she adds a new addition to the mix—six month old baby Keegan.

Martin further demonstrates her writing versatility with fantasy books. One of her earliest, *Ma and Pa Dracula*, was released in 1989. Fantasy writing is a far cry from Martin's more realistic Baby-sitters Club novels where her plots contain normal, everyday conflicts, and her characters have the potential to be real people. *The Doll People*—the first in a series of three fantasy books written with the help of Henry Holt's editor-in-chief of children's books, Laura Godwin—provides a good illustration of Martin's imagination.

As little girls, Martin and Godwin believed that their dolls came to life when there were no human beings around. In the first book, *The Doll People*, the authors wove a tale of two doll families, the antique Dolls, of which Annabelle is part, and the modern, plastic Funcraft family with Tiffany. The dolls live with two sisters, Kate and Nora Palmer. In the sequel, *The Meanest Doll in the World,* published in 2003, the dolls are carried by mistake to another home where they encounter a princess doll who is indeed, the meanest doll in the world. To create the Doll People series, which also consists of the forthcoming, *The Runaway Dolls*, each author took on specific assignments. Laura is credited with the basic idea for the book's characters and plot, and both authors contribute to the outlining of the stories, the writing, and the editing. All of the Doll People books are illustrated by Brian Selznick.

Book reviewers thought Martin and Laura made a good team. *Publishers Weekly* said: "Martin and Godwin inventively spin out their own variation on the perennially popular theme of toys who secretly come to life . . . [t]he authors provide plenty of action and suspense, yet it is their skillfully crafted details about the dolls' personalities and daily routines that prove most memorable."[60]

School Library Journal said of *The Runaway Dolls*, "This fantasy with its broad humor, evil machinations, and tales of friendship will delight both fans of the *Doll People* and those new to the story . . ."[61]

In addition to writing chapter books, Martin has also demonstrated her creativity by producing illustrated books. In 1983, Martin co-wrote *My Puppy Scrapbook Featuring Fenwick* with Betsy Ryan. The book was illustrated by Martin's father, Henry (Hank) Martin. (He has also illustrated some of the Baby-sitters Club books, in addition to Martin's *Moving Day in Feathertown* and *Fancy Dance in Feather*

Town, both published in 1988). In 1996, Martin released *Leo the Magnificat*, illustrated by Caldecott Medal winner, Emily Arnold McCully. In this book, Martin tells the story of a cat who adopts a church congregation in Louisville, Kentucky, and lives in the church for 12 years. When Leo

Did you know...

Ann M. Martin is frequently asked about her writing techniques and how to write well. Here are "Ann's Top Ten Writing Tips." The list is posted on a Scholastic Books Website (*www.scholastic.com/annmartin/letters/ online051001.htm*).

1. Practice. Write something every day.
2. Read as much as you can—it's one of the best ways to become a better writer.
3. Write about something that interests you.
4. Find a comfortable place to write and get into a routine. Try to write every day whether you feel like it or not.
5. Think of an interesting way to start your writing; something that will capture the interest of your reader.
6. Keep at it. Don't quit
7. Revise and edit your work.
8. Don't be afraid of writers block. When it happens, walk away from your writing and come back to it later.
9. Ask for advice. Start a writers' group with some friends and share your writing.
10. Take a creative writing class, if you can.

dies, he is given a proper funeral complete with burial in the church garden. Reviewers said of Martin's *Leo the Magnificat*: "Martin has a knack for knowing how youngsters think and express themselves . . . She is especially adept at conveying emotion, an important part of the sentimental story."[62]

Martin has won many awards for her writing. Four of her books have been chosen Children's Books of the Year by the Child Study Association of America, an organization that promotes the understanding of child development, and works to better relationships between parents and children. The recognized books are: *Inside Out, Stage Fright, With You and Without You*, and *Missing Since Monday*.

Martin has never written nonfiction nor has she written for adults; she only writes fictional stories for young readers. About writing fiction she says:

> One interesting thing about writing [fiction] is that when you're making up a story, you're in charge. You can solve problems the way you wish they could be solved in real life. It's a way to work out the "if onlys" and the "what ifs." The "if onlys" are all the things you think about, all the solutions to problems in your own life that you didn't come up with fast enough. You know—when something happens in school and later that night you think, Oh, if only I had said this or that. Well, when you're writing, you can say or do those things. And the "what ifs" are simply anything you can imagine. You can have fun playing out all those scenes and situations you might like to see happen in real life—and those things you wouldn't like to see happen, as well. The "what-ifs" are your creative mind at work.[63]

Martin sees her writing as an opportunity to "remember, relive and redo"[64] events that have happened in her life, making it possible to experience the "if onlys" firsthand.

Martin always revises her work; sometimes it takes two or three revisions and sometimes it only takes one. She said:

> Writing can be hard work but mostly it feels exciting, especially when I'm very involved with the characters or the scene. I can feel the excitement in my stomach. It's almost like being at the circus.[65]

Martin's favorite book, of all that she has written, constantly changes. She finds it hard to let go of a book once it has been published, so usually her latest book remains her favorite, until another book is released. One book, however, came to mean more to her than any of the others, as much for its autobiographical content as for the recognition it would receive. That book is *A Corner of the Universe*.

Ann M. Martin's book A Corner of the Universe *was designated a Newbery Honor Book. The Newbery Medal was named after John Newbery. It is a prestigious award given by the Association for Library Service to Children (ALSC), a division of the American Library Association (ALA), to the author of the most distinguished contribution to American literature for children. Here, at the Mid-Winter meeting of the ALA in January 2004, ALSC President Cynthia Richey awards the Newbery Medal to Kate DiCamillo for her book* The Tale of Despereaux.

6

Winning a Newbery Honor

ONE EARLY MORNING in the beginning of 2003, Martin received a phone call. It was a member of the American Library Association (ALA) calling to inform her that her book, *A Corner of the Universe*, had been designated a Newbery Honor Book.

The Newbery Medal, which is awarded annually by the American Library Association, honors outstanding children's books that have been published in the United States during the previous year. The Newbery Medal award-winning books are considered the most prestigious chapter books for young readers. (Outstanding picture books published in any given year are recognized by a separate award—the Randolf Caldecott Medal.) Each year the Newbery Medal award-winning book is selected by a special committee of children's librarians called the Newbery committee. Committee members read hundreds of books before selecting one to receive the Newbery Medal. When evaluating a book, they study its concept, organization, plot development, setting, and characterization. They also review the author's overall style of writing.

The Newbery Medal award is named after John Newbery, an 18th-century British publisher and bookseller who was an early advocate of children's literacy. Newbery is believed to be the first person to publish and sell books for children. He is also credited with being the first to recognize that children's books have an entertainment value. Prior to Newbery, the main focus of children's books was educational. In 1744, Newbery published *A Pretty Little Pocket Book*, thought to be the first children's book ever published. Newbery also published the first magazine for children, *The Lilliputian Magazine*, in 1751. In 1921, the American Library Association began recognizing authors of children's literature by awarding a medal in honor of John Newbery.

Frederic G. Melcher (1872–1963), editor of *Publishers Weekly* and a co-founder of Children's Book Week (usually held in November), was one of the promoters of the Newbery Medal award. He believed that recognition of outstanding works of children's literature would "encourage original creative work in the field of books for children."[66] In addition, in promoting the award, Melcher believed it would ". . . emphasize to the public that contributions to the literature for children deserve similar recognition to poetry, plays, or novels. To give those librarians, who make it their life work to serve children's reading interests, an opportunity to encourage good writing in this field."[67]

Only one book per calendar year is selected to be a New-bery Medal award winner. However, the founders of the award recognized that in any given year, there could be other books worthy of a Newbery Medal. At first these books were referred to as "Newbery runners-up." In 1972, the phrase "runners up" was changed to "honor books," and all of the former "Newbery runners up" books were then known as Newbery Honor books.

Did you know...

Ann M. Martin's favorite character from the Baby-sitters Club series is Kristy Thomas—the girl who has the idea for the club. Martin likes Kristy because she is outspoken and has her own ideas. A poll of readers by Scholastic Books, however, shows that read-ers voted Stacey McGill as the most-popular character of the series.

Martin is often asked to name her favorite book of the series. She says that while she was writing the books, her favorite was number 6, *Kristy's Big Day*. However, now that she has finished the series, her favorite is *Kristy's Big Idea*, the book that set every-thing in motion.

From all the books Martin has written, her favorite character is Annabelle Doll from *The Doll People* and its sequels. Martin favors Annabelle because she loves fantasy.

Of all the characters Martin has created, Hattie Owen—from Martin's Newbery Honor winner *A Corner of the Universe*—is the most autobiographical.

The first Newbery Medal was awarded in 1922 to *The Story of Mankind* by the American author and journalist, Hendrik Willem van Loon (1882–1944). In recent years, the award has been presented to such distinguished authors as Louis Sachar for *Holes*, Linda Sue Park for *A Single Shard*, Katherine Paterson for *Bridge to Terabithia* and *Jacob Have I Loved*, and Lois Lowry for *The Giver*.

The Newbery Medal winner for 2003, the year Martin's *A Corner of the Universe* won the Newbery Honor, was *Crispin: The Cross of Lead* by Avi. Sharing the Newbery Honor with *A Corner of the Universe* in 2003 were: *The House of the Scorpion* by Nancy Farmer, *Pictures of Hollis Woods* by Patricia Reilly Giff, *Hoot* by Carl Hiaasen, and *Surviving the Applewhites* by Stephanie S. Tolan.

The Association for Library Service to Children, a division of the American Library Association publicly announced the Newbery Medal, Newbery Honor, and Caldecott Medal winners during the American Library Association's midwinter meeting in Philadelphia, January 24–29, 2003. As soon as the word was out, Martin's phone rang constantly with calls of congratulations and well-wishes from her many friends in the children's writing and publishing world.

Winning a Newbery Medal is an honor any author would be proud of. For Martin it was an extraordinary honor. ". . . Newbery books have always been special to me," Martin posted on the Scholastic Books website. "I was a big reader as a child, and when I saw a gold-embossed Newbery sticker on a book in my library, I'd usually add the book to the must-read stack I was collecting to go home with me. I never imagined that one day a sticker would be on a book I'd written . . ."[68]

A Corner of the Universe has special meaning to Martin,

aside from being a Newbery Honor book. While not entirely autographical, it is based, in part, on events that occurred in Martin's family. *A Corner of the Universe* relates the story of young Hattie Owens, whose uncle, Adam, is mentally ill. Like Hattie, Martin had a mentally ill uncle; her mother's brother, Stephen, whom she never met, suffered from schizophrenia. Hattie's Uncle Adam is based on Martin's Uncle Stephen. Stephen committed suicide when he was 23 years old, a few years before Martin's parents met. In the book, Adam also kills himself.

Martin did not even know she had an Uncle Stephen until she was 9 years old. "I remember that what surprised me more than the existence of this uncle and the story behind him was the fact that he had been kept a secret," Martin explained.[69] Even after she knew about her uncle, his suicide was not something her family talked a lot about while she was growing up, and it was not until she was in her 40s that she decided to write about it. She was inspired to do so when, while getting ready to transfer some home movies onto video tape as a present for her sister, Jane, Martin came across old movies of her Uncle Stephen.

Martin did not tell anyone in the family about *A Corner of the Universe* until the book was almost finished. She was not sure what their response would be to hearing that she had written about a family secret. By then, Martin's mother, Edie, was suffering from Alzheimer's disease and was not able to discuss the book with her, but Martin did share the story with her father, Hank, and cousin. She was surprised that they were both very supportive of her telling the story. Martin found that through writing *A Corner of the Universe* she learned a lot about herself.

Martin found it both easier and more difficult to write a book that was inspired by her own life. "It made it easier in

In A Corner of the Universe, *Ann M. Martin modeled the mentally ill character after her real uncle, who suffered from schizophrenia. The book dealt with some of Martin's personal family issues like mental illness and suicide. Public awareness of schizophrenia increased following the release of the film* A Beautiful Mind, *which chronicled the brilliant, yet difficult, life of math prodigy John Nash. Here we see a clip from the film in which actor Russell Crowe (seated) portrays the brilliant Nash.*

that the story was personal to me, that I had a very easy time finding my way into Hattie's head," Martin told a group of third graders in an online interview. "But it was difficult because I wasn't sure how my family was going to react to it."[70]

"Even though I never met my Uncle Stephen, the book seemed more personal to me than my others—more steeped in family history," said Martin. "I hope readers come away [from reading *A Corner of the Universe*] thinking about people they've known—who are a little off center—with more openness and warmth, knowing that the same basic human feelings are attached to everyone."[71]

Martin received her Newbery Honor award at a special awards ceremony held by the American Library Association in Toronto later that year. On the night before she was to receive the award, Scholastic Inc., *A Corner of the Universe*'s publisher, held a party in Martin's honor. They turned an indoor space into a carnival similar to the one that visits Hattie's hometown in the book. Hundreds of people attended. They rode a life-size Ferris wheel (like the one on the cover of the book), played for prizes at booths where wheels of fortune spun out lucky numbers, ate carnival food, and had their fortunes told by a fortune teller.

Over 500 people attended the American Library Association banquet the next evening, when Martin received her award. She had the opportunity to speak personally with and thank the members of the Newbery Committee that had selected *A Corner of the Universe* as a Newbery Honor book.

Martin summed up the honor for her readers when she posted the following on the Scholastic Books website: "Maybe years from now while browsing through the library, a reader will see the Newbery Honor sticker on *A Corner of the Universe*. And just like me when I was young, she'll decide that she simply has to add it to her stack of 'must read' books."[72]

As the Baby-sitters Club series grew in popularity, so, too, did its marketing momentum. One such marketing idea was The Baby-sitters Club Mystery Game, pictured here.

Ann and Paula

WHEN MARTIN FIRST began writing the Baby-sitter Club series, she became pen pals with some of her readers. (These girls are now in their 20s, and some have children of their own.) One of Martin's pen pals was a girl named Kathy Ames. A friendship grew out of Kathy and Martin's correspondence, which eventually led to occasional dinner meetings in New York City. When the late Paula Danziger, author of the Amber Brown series and other books, visited Kathy's school, Kathy asked her if she had ever met Ann M. Martin. Paula admitted she never had, and asked Kathy to tell Martin to contact her, which Kathy did. Martin called Paula and left a message on her answering machine, inviting her to dinner. Paula thought Martin had a "really sweet voice"[73] and a few weeks later, the two authors met. A close friendship immediately formed.

Paula and Martin found they had more in common than being best-selling authors of children's books. They both started their professional careers as teachers. As writers, each felt a responsibility to their craft, and understood the other's need to produce good literature for young readers. Both authors wanted to tackle sensitive and difficult subjects in their books, and neither was afraid to do so. Paula and Martin also shared a silly sense of humor, and birthdays that fell in August (Paula's birthday was August 18).

The two authors were also different in many ways, and their differences made their friendship even stronger. Martin is an animal lover and Paula was allergic to animals. Martin is shy and becomes nervous when speaking in front of a crowd; Paula had her own British television show called *Alive and Kicking*. Martin is an accomplished seamstress and needle worker; Paula hated to sew. Paula was talkative while Martin is quiet. Paula loved to shop; Martin does not enjoy shopping. Paula once explained her friendship with Martin this way:

> [Martin] has a real heart about things. She cares. She's a good friend to call when I'm having problems with dating, hair, clothing choices, and other world-shattering issues. Like dust in my contact lenses. I can also count on her to call me when she's terrified of a spider she's found in her house, when her cats do something she thinks is funny, and when she wants to tell me about an *I Love Lucy* episode she's just seen for the eightieth time . . . . I've also learned a lot from Annie about helping others, and I'm very glad she's my friend (even at three in the morning when the spider shows up).[74]

One of their most noticeable differences was the way they dressed. Paula loved to dress in a flamboyant way with wildly—colored scarves and purple nail polish. Martin is, and always has been, a much more conservative dresser. Paula once described the friends' first meeting at Scholastic Inc. to propose their idea of writing *P.S. Longer Letter Later*. She said, "Ann was dressed in plain corduroy pants and a shirt that looked like something the *Where's Waldo?* guy would wear. I was wearing glitter Doc Martens, a sweeping dress and a sparkly scarf."[75]

Did you know...

Scholastic Books maintains a Website for Ann M. Martin, where she regularly posts letters to her readers about a variety of subjects.

Sometimes Martin writes about current happenings in her life, such as what she did over the holidays or what book she is working on at the moment. Other times she writes about what is going on in the world—after September 11, 2001, Martin posted a letter reassuring her readers that the United States was going to be okay. In one of the entries, Martin interviews the late author Paula Danziger and Danziger interviews Martin.

These letters date back to January 2000, and reading them is a great way to glimpse little snap-shot portraits of Martin's life. The Website's address is *www.scholastic.com/annmartin/letters/index.htm*.

The two authors had been friends for nearly a decade before they began writing together. Martin and Paula shared the same agent, who suggested the initial collaboration. Henry Holt editor, Laura Godwin, Martin's co-author of *The Doll People*, was also a mutual friend of both Martin and Paula. She came up with the idea of *P.S. Longer Letter Later* when she suggested the two write a book using an exchange of letters between two 11-year-old girls. The fictional girls, like Martin and Paula, were friends despite being opposites in a lot of ways. Laura suggested each author write as one of the girls, and put some of her own personality into her character. In this way, Paula became Tara*Starr, a whimsical free sprit and Martin became the character of shy and reserved Elizabeth. After being friends for years, the girls are separated when Tara*Starr's family moves to Ohio. Elizabeth is at first the more stable character, but as the book progresses, Tara*Starr's family situation improves and Elizabeth's falls apart as her father loses his job and has a nervous breakdown. Martin came up with the title; it came from the many fan letters that she received that ended with the words, "P.S. Longer Letter Later."

With the characters and plot in place, Martin and Paula began corresponding by fax machine. Martin, as Elizabeth, would write a letter and fax it off to Paula, who would answer it as Tara*Starr. Their characters grew as the book took shape.

Both Martin and Paula found collaboration to be challenging. "We were able to write on our own and yet work together," said Paula, who admitted she missed not having complete control over the book.[76] She said:

> I think the reason *P.S. Longer Letter Later* worked was the
> fact that we each had our own voice. Ann is more serious and

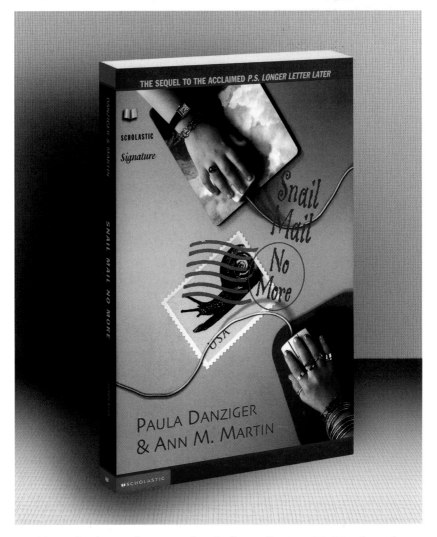

Writing a book together proved a challenge for Ann M. Martin and
Paula Danziger because neither author had ever co-authored a book. In
the end, their efforts paid off, and in 1999 they published P.S. Longer
Letter Later. *A year later, the co-authors wrote the pictured book,*
Snail Mail No More, *as a sequel to* P.S. Longer Letter Later.

I am more outspoken, I love play. We were able to say something about friendship and differences.[77]

For Martin, writing without a detailed outline was a new

experience for her. When the authors had different views on how the story should progress, they integrated the disagreement into the plot. "In a way, we became Tara*Starr and Elizabeth, and argued things out the way they would," said Martin.[78]

P.S. Longer Letter Later was published in 1999. As eighth graders, Tara*Starr and Elizabeth continued their correspondence by e-mail in *Snail Mail No More*, which was published in 2000.

P.S. Longer Letter Later and *Snail Mail No More* resulted in the outstanding combination of two extraordinary authors, a fact that reviewers duly noted. Of *P.S. Longer Letter Later*, the *New York Times* wrote that the book is ". . . a spirited and readable book . . . a lively and engaging 234-page duet without a sour note."[79]

Of the sequel, a reviewer for *Booklist* stated: "seasoned pros Danziger and Martin couldn't write a dull book if they tried and this one . . . is a funny, thought-provoking page-turner that will delight readers and leave them ready for more messages."[80]

"Students will identify with the two teenagers and their struggles of friendship," said *School Library Journal* about *Snail Mail No More*.[81]

After the release of *Snail Mail No More*, the authors toyed with the idea of writing a third book about the characters, but they came to an agreement that there would be no more books about Elizabeth and Tara*Starr. "It's Tara and Elizabeth No More," said Paula.[82]

Although there was no way to know at the time Paula said those words, the "no more" would apply not only to books about Elizabeth and Tara*Starr, but to any future collaborations between Martin and Paula. In June of 2004, Paula suffered two heart attacks and died in a New York hospital on

July 8, 2004. She was 59 years old. At the time of her death she had written over 30 books and was the recipient of many literary awards, including the Children's Choice Award.

A few months after Paula's death, Martin posted a passage about her friend on the Scholastic Books website:

> I'm left with memories of my funny, smart, and talented friend. I'm especially grateful for the time we shared writing *P.S. Longer Letter Later* and *Snail Mail No More*. It's impossible to think of Paula without remembering her boundless energy and enthusiasm. She loved to travel, she loved meeting new people and she loved her readers. She also had a sense of style that was all her own. I'm guessing that Paula wouldn't want anybody to be sad now. In fact, I think it's safe to say that Paula would wish for all her fans to pick up a good book, make a new friend, and maybe even put on some purple nail polish and a wild, colorful outfit in her honor.[83]

Ann M. Martin has always been generous. She has founded and supports count-less organizations, including the Make-A-Wish Foundation, which grants wishes to ill children. Disney is one of the foundation's greatest supporters, hosting fundraisers and events for the benefiting children. Shown above at a fundraiser aboard Disney's Magic *cruise ship in 2005, from Mickey Mouse on the left to Minnie Mouse on the right, are Disney CEO elect Bob Iger, Make-A-Wish Foundation CEO David Williams, and Disney CEO Michael Eisner.*

8

A Generous Woman

THE STRONG SENSE of volunteerism that her parents had instilled in her as a child has remained with Martin throughout the years. She continues to volunteer and give back to the community, and she believes that all young people have the potential to be good at giving back to the community once they know where to start. She tells them:

> I think one of the easiest ways to get involved (at any age) is in your own neighborhood. Perhaps there are elderly neighbors who need their grass mowed, their sidewalk shoveled, or someone to stop in for an occasional visit . . . You don't have to go very far from home to make a difference![84]

In 1990, Martin made a public gesture of generosity when she founded the Ann M. Martin Foundation. The purpose of the foundation is to give financial support to organizations that help children, literacy programs, and homeless people and animals. The Ann M. Martin Foundation also funds organizations that have a special interest in children's art programs. In addition, it awards a select number of private and parochial school scholarships each year to students at the grade school, college, and post-graduate levels, and maintains support for as long as the student wishes to continue his or her education. The Ann M. Martin Foundation is funded by Martin personally, and by the proceeds she receives from the sale of merchandise based on her books. Martin is the president of the foundation, and her sister, Jane, is the vice-president. Martin believes that the Ann M. Martin Foundation is one of the best things to have come from her writing success.

Now a wealthy woman, Martin is very generous. She said:

> Having money doesn't matter much to me, except for two things—being able to give it away through the foundation, and just being comfortable. I can remember . . . lying in bed one morning and wondering if I'd be able to pay my electric bill that month . . . . It's really nice not to have to worry about things like that now.[85]

Christmas was always a special time when Martin was growing up and she wants those in need to be able to experience the same special joy that the holiday can bring. Each December she purchases gifts for homeless or underprivileged kids. This volunteer activity brings as much joy to Martin as it does the recipients of the presents. She is given the age and sex of each child on the list, and then she has a wonderful time going up and down the aisles of a big toy store looking for toys, games, dolls, art supplies, and stuffed animals that she thinks the kids will enjoy. According to Martin, helping others puts your own needs into perspective.

Martin also turns book signings into an opportunity to help those in need. When she visits book stores, Scholastic Inc. runs a promotion which invites children to take on projects

Did you know...

Ann M. Martin used the revenue generated by the Baby-sitters Club books as well as from related merchandise to start the Ann M. Martin Foundation. The original four Baby-Sitters Club books grew to close to 400 volumes by the time the series was ended in 2000. In addition to the 132 books in the Baby-sitters Club series, there are

- 120 books in the Baby-sitters Little Sisters series;
- 6 books in the Baby-sitters Little Sisters Super Special series;
- 36 books in the Baby-sitters Mysteries series;
- 13 books in the Baby-sitters Super Specials series;
- 3 books in the Baby-sitters Super Mysteries series;
- 6 books in the Baby-sitters Club Portrait Collection series;
- 12 books in the Baby-sitters Club Friends Forever series;
- 2 books in the Baby-sitters Club Friends Forever Special series;
- 12 books in the Kids in Ms. Coleman's Class series;
- 16 books in the Baby-sitter Club Special Edition series; and
- 15 books in the California Diaries series.
Total number of books: 373.

that benefit the community. For example, the book store may run a food drive and ask everyone who comes to see Martin to bring a can of food. "I think it's important that kids become aware that they can make a difference, whether it's by donating time or skills, their allowance or a can of food, or by reaching into other people's lives in their own personal way," explained Martin.[86] Martin also invites the book stores she visits to pick a local nonprofit agency to be the recipient of a grant from the Ann M. Martin Foundation.

Another way Martin has given back to the community is through the Adopt-a-School Program. This program is associated with the National Dance Institute, which was started in 1976 by former New York City Ballet dancer Jacques D'Amboise. The National Dance Institute brings dance to inner city school children. Jacques believes that learning to dance develops excellence in other areas of a child's life. Each September, dance teachers visit New York City schools (and schools in other cities) and hold auditions for students who would like to take part in the National Dance Program. Thousands of children participate, and at the end of the year, a large production is staged. The program, which Martin believes is a great self-esteem builder for children, was initially funded by government and local funding. When the funding was decreased in the 1980s, private funding was needed, and Martin, along with other generous benefactors, stepped in and financially adopted specific schools to help keep the program running. Martin's "adoptee" was Public School (PS) 2 in New York City's Chinatown, which as it turned out, had an Ann M. Martin fan club. Martin once said she felt as adopted by the children in PS 2 as the school did by her. Martin often stopped by PS 2 to speak with the children, and watch rehearsals. Each June, Martin eagerly looked forward to attending the Big Performance when all

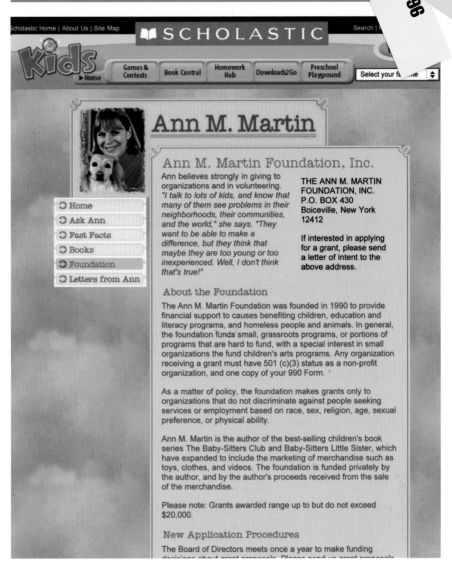

Scholastic Home | About Us | Site Map

▐ SCHOLASTIC

Search |

Kids
▶ Home | Games & Contests | Book Central | Homework Hub | Downloads2Go | Preschool Playground | Select your fa...me ⬍

Ann M. Martin

Ann M. Martin Foundation, Inc.

○ Home
○ Ask Ann
○ Fast Facts
○ Books
○ Foundation
○ Letters from Ann

Ann believes strongly in giving to organizations and in volunteering. *"I talk to lots of kids, and know that many of them see problems in their neighborhoods, their communities, and the world,"* she says. *"They want to be able to make a difference, but they think that maybe they are too young or too inexperienced. Well, I don't think that's true!"*

THE ANN M. MARTIN FOUNDATION, INC.
P.O. BOX 430
Boiceville, New York 12412

If interested in applying for a grant, please send a letter of intent to the above address.

About the Foundation

The Ann M. Martin Foundation was founded in 1990 to provide financial support to causes benefiting children, education and literacy programs, and homeless people and animals. In general, the foundation funds small, grassroots programs, or portions of programs that are hard to fund, with a special interest in small organizations the fund children's arts programs. Any organization receiving a grant must have 501 (c)(3) status as a non-profit organization, and one copy of your 990 Form. '

As a matter of policy, the foundation makes grants only to organizations that do not discriminate against people seeking services or employment based on race, sex, religion, age, sexual preference, or physical ability.

Ann M. Martin is the author of the best-selling children's book series The Baby-Sitters Club and Baby-Sitters Little Sister, which have expanded to include the marketing of merchandise such as toys, clothes, and videos. The foundation is funded privately by the author, and by the author's proceeds received from the sale of the merchandise.

Please note: Grants awarded range up to but do not exceed $20,000.

New Application Procedures

The Board of Directors meets once a year to make funding

Scholastic Inc. supports the Ann M. Martin Foundation Website. Martin is the president of this foundation, which she founded in 1990 to provide financial support to various causes.

the New York City students in the program performed together.

Another cause that is near and dear to Martin is the Lisa Novak Community Libraries, an organization which she helped co-found. The organization was started in memory of Martin's friend, Lisa Novak, a children's book editor, who was killed while on vacation in 1990. After Lisa died, Martin and Lisa's other friends from the writing and publishing community wanted to do something to honor their friend. They created the Lisa Libraries as a way of bringing together Lisa's love of reading and her passion for children's literature. The Lisa Libraries builds or supplements small children's libraries in communities where there is a lack of books. The organization also provides new books to day care centers, after-school programs, community centers and state prisons with children's visiting areas. Because of the Lisa Libraries, children who may otherwise never own a book get one, or several, of their own.

To acquire books for the Lisa Libraries, Martin asked editors, authors, book reviewers, and publishers to donate their extra copies. Over the years, publications such as *Publishers Weekly* have donated thousands of books to the Lisa Libraries. After they are donated, the books are sorted into categories and packed into boxes. They are then sent to agencies who request them. At first Martin ran the Lisa Libraries out of her spare Manhattan apartment bedroom; now the books are warehoused in Brooklyn, New York. In 2004, 15,000 books went out to nonprofit agencies across the United States. Martin hopes the "the Lisa Libraries will go on for many, many years to come, continuing with its goal to put new books into the hands of eager young readers."[87]

One of the programs associated with the Lisa Libraries is Reach Out and Read, which started in Boston in 1989. Reach Out and Read coordinates children's literacy with pediatric medical care. When a child sees a Reach Out and Read-associated doctor for a well-child checkup, he or she also receives a book to take home and keep. This happens at every well-child doctor's office visit from the time the child is 6 months until he or she is 5 years old. The child's parents are given "doctor's orders" to read to their child every day. Parents also receive information about the importance of reading and the role it plays in the language development of their children.

There are more than 180 Reach Out and Read sites in clinics and pediatrician's offices in 39 states across America. The Reach Out and Read program in Martin's home state of New York began in December 1998. First Lady Hillary Clinton was present at the launch. The Lisa Libraries and Reach Out and Read partnership began the following September, in 1999. Today the Lisa Libraries supplies picture and board books to the Reach Out and Read program. Together the two agencies administer the Reach Out and Read program to over 30,000 children each year. "[It makes me happy] knowing that another child will fall asleep tonight after hearing his or her favorite bedtime story. I *love* kids, I *love* to read, and I *love* having my very own books, so you can see why I'm a big fan of Reach Out and Read," Martin posted on the Scholastic Books website.[88]

Martin has also been a contributor to Save the Children—an international charity that helps children living in poverty—and the Make-A-Wish Foundation and the Starlight Foundation—two organizations that grant wishes to seriously ill children. She also helps her four-legged friends. An animal lover to the core, Martin serves as a volunteer for the Animal Welfare and Adoption Network (AWAN), a nonprofit organization that asks volunteer to offer temporary shelter to abandoned animals. She accepts cats and kittens from AWAN into her home and foster mothers them until they are can be adopted into permanent homes.

Here Ann M. Martin is seen at a bookstore in Albuquerque, New Mexico, signing her latest Baby-sitters Club book for fans in 1997. That year, the series was 12 years old and still popular with teen girls and young women who remembered the books as youth classics.

9

"An Incredible Adventure"

MARTIN HAS NEVER been one to chase after fame and fortune, and it was never her intention to start a publishing phenomenon when she began writing the Baby-sitters Club books in 1985. Nevertheless, over the years, Martin's hard work and amazing success as an author have brought along with them their own financial rewards. There are those who would say she leads a charmed life, but Martin tries not to let her celebrity and good fortune change the way she lives. When she is asked to describe herself, Martin says she is a "homebody"—and although she loves people, especially her fans and children in general, she likes living a simple, quiet life, socializing only with her family and close friends. She has never married and has no children, but she has "many, many godchildren."[89] She likes being around other people, but she is also happy when she is alone, and prefers a quiet atmosphere to a noisy gathering or party.

As a best-selling author, Martin is often asked to speak in public. She is better today at giving presentations than she was back in grade school; however, she still gets nervous once in a while. Martin says:

> I turned to writing as an outlet for both my emotions and humor. I feel I'm more articulate and funnier on paper, but the more I write, the more comfortable I become speaking. It's a delightfully vicious cycle. The marriage of my love for children's literature with this cycle makes for a continually gratifying creative process.[90]

For many years, Martin owned a co-op apartment in Manhattan, New York. Now she lives in a large, 14-room farmhouse in the Catskill Mountains in Ulster County in upstate New York. Most days she can be found working on her books in the farmhouse's attic, which she has turned into her office. From its windows, Martin can see the mountains and a lake. In keeping with her simple life on the farm, Martin is most comfortable when dressed casually, in jeans and sneakers. She is a vegetarian, and she enjoys gardening and growing vegetables on her property such as cucumbers, tomatoes, eggplants, peppers, and others. The picturesque area in which she lives allows Martin to indulge her love of nature. She loves to be outdoors during all four seasons, but she especially loves winter and snow.

The creativity inspired by her parents has stayed with Martin into her adult years, and she spends her free time doing the things she enjoyed as a child. She still loves to knit and sew; she makes clothes for the children of her friends. She also likes creating greeting cards.

Ann M. Martin treasures her privacy, preferring to spend time writing and doing crafts rather than attending parties. Although the Baby-sitters Club series has ended, Martin continues to write for young adults. Here Martin is playing with her cat named Mouse in her apartment in New York.

Although she has a busy career as a writer, Martin has never lost her childhood love of reading. She tries to read as often as she can, and participates in a local book club, when time will allow. Martin enjoys reading books that have realistic plots and those that contain events that could happen in everyday life. She also likes scary stories—Stephen King is one of her favorite authors. Among her favorite adult books are *To Kill a Mockingbird* by Harper Lee and *The Heart Is a Lonely Hunter* by Carson McCullers.

Another aspect of her childhood that has remained with Martin over the years is her love of animals. Animals continue to play a big role in Martin's life. Currently, Martin has three cats—Gussie, Woody, and Willy. Martin likes cats because they are so responsive:

. . . . Cats definitely have their own opinions. And they have sense of humor . . . my cats make me laugh, and I'm pretty sure that sometimes they do it on purpose . . . . also, they're very affectionate, which is nice.[91]

Martin also has a dog named Sadie, who is a beagle–golden retriever mix and the first dog she has ever owned. Martin got Sadie when she was a puppy in 1998; she was one from a litter born to an abandoned pregnant mother rescued by the Animal Welfare and Adoption Network.

Martin continues to maintain a demanding writing schedule; she has two books scheduled to be released in 2005. *A Dog's Life: the Autobiography of a Stray* is a tale about two puppies who must make it in the big world on their own. Martin is also planning a continuation of the adventures of Annabelle and Tiffany in *The Runaway Dolls*, the third book

Did you know...

Ann M. Martin has always completed the research necessary to insure that her books are not only realistic, but factually accurate. For example, when she wrote about diabetes in The Baby-sitters Club book, *The Truth About Stacey*, Martin thoroughly researched the disease and had a doctor review her manuscript prior to publication. Interestingly, after reading Martin's accurate description of diabetes in *The Truth About Stacey*, one young reader recognized the diabetic symptoms that she was experiencing and she was soon diagnosed with juvenile diabetes. Many other young people have written to Martin to tell her that *The Truth About Stacey* has helped them explain their disease to their friends.

in the Doll People series. Like the previous two books in the series, *The Runaway Dolls* is co-written with Laura Godwin and illustrated by Brian Selznick.

Even though the Baby-sitters Club books are no longer being produced, they are still popular with young readers. However, there are no plans for resuming the Baby-sitters Club books or any of the related series at this time. Nor are there plans for a "Baby-sitters Reunion," although Martin thinks it is a good idea and does not rule out the possibility.

Martin wants to continue writing for many years to come, and hopes never to retire. She feels very lucky to have been given the opportunity to create the characters that so many readers have come to love. She does not consider herself to be famous, but she does enjoy going to bookstores and seeing her books on the shelves and meeting readers and receiving letters from them. Martin receives well over 1,000 fan letters a month. To Martin, contact with her readers is one of the best things about being an author.

Martin wants her young readers to understand that the phenomenal writing achievement she enjoys is not the norm for most authors. She says:

> I think kids should realize that this is a sort of fairy tale, and that it doesn't happen to most people who set out to write books. There are many excellent writers who earn a nice living. But an awful lot of writers hold down a second job to support themselves. Something like this is really unusual and lucky.[92]

Fame and fortune are not Martin's definition of success. To her, success is doing the best, and being the best at whatever you want to do. Martin never expected half the things that her gift of writing has brought into her life, but she has enjoyed the "incredible adventure,"[93] and she looks forward with anticipation, to what the future will bring.

1 Margot Becker R. and *Ann M. Martin, Ann M. Martin: The Story of the Author of the Baby-sitters Club* (New York: Scholastic Inc., 1993), 127.

2 Ann M. Martin, "Fast Facts," Scholastic Canada: Ann Martin, *www.scholastic.ca/authors/ martin_a/facts.htm.*

3 N.R. Kleinfield, "Children's Books: Inside the Baby-Sitters Club," *New York Times Book Review*, April 30, 1989, 42.

4 Heidi Henneman, "Bye-bye to The Baby-Sitters Club," BookPage Interview January 2001: Ann Martin, *www.book- page.com/0101bp/ann_ martin.html.*

5 Ibid.

6 Ann M. Martin, "Where do I Get My Ideas?" Ann M. Martin: Letters from Ann, *www.scholas- tic.com/annmartin/letters/ online0301.htm.*

7 Ann M. Martin, "Goodbye BSC!" Ann M. Martin: Letters from Ann, *www.scholastic.com/ annmartin/letters/online1200.htm.*

8 Henneman, "Bye-bye to The Baby-Sitters Club."

9 Kleinfield, "Children's Books: Inside the Baby-Sitters Club."

10 Quoted in Ann Cammire, ed., "Ann M. Martin," *Children's Literature Review* Vol. 32 (Detroit, MI: Gale Research, 1986), 195.

11 Kristin McMurran, "Ann Martin Stirs Up a Tiny Tempest in Preteen Land with her Best-

selling Baby-sitters Club," *People Weekly*, August 21, 1989, 55.

12 Henneman, "Bye-bye to The Baby-Sitters Club."

13 Martin, "Goodbye BSC!"

14 Ibid.

15 R. and Martin, *Ann M. Martin: The Story of the Author of The Baby-sitters Club*, 147.

16 Henneman, "Bye-bye to the Baby-Sitters Club."

17 Ann M. Martin, *Graduation Day* (New York, NY: Scholastic Inc., 2000), 183.

18 Martin, "Goodbye BSC!"

19 R. and Martin, Ann M. Martin: *The Story of the Author of The Baby-sitters Club*, 24.

20 Ann M. Martin, "Ann M. Martin's Biography," Scholastic.com | AuthorsandBooks: Author Booklist, *www2.scholastic.com/teachers/ authorsandbooks/authorstudies/ authorhome.jhtml?authorID=57& collateralID=5225&displayName =Biography.*

21 Susan Ferraro, "Girl Talk," *New York Times*, December 5, 1992, 62.

22 Quoted in Ann Cammire, ed., *Something about the Author* Vol. 44 (Detroit: Gale Research, 1986), 115.

23 Ann M. Martin, "Family/Friend Game Night," Ann M. Martin: Letters from Ann, *www.scholas- tic.com/annmartin/letters/online2 _1_00.htm.*

24 McMurran, "Ann Martin Stirs Up a Tiny Tempest in Preteen Land

with her Best-selling Baby-sitters Club," 55.

25 R. and Martin, *Ann M. Martin: The Story of the Author of The Baby-sitters Club*, 50.

26 Ibid., 33.

27 Ibid., 35.

28 Quoted in Sally Holmes Holtze, ed., *Seventh Book of Junior Authors and Illustrators* (Bronx, NY: The H.W. Wilson Company, 1996).

29 R. and Martin, *Ann M. Martin: The Story of the Author of the Baby-sitters Club*, 56.

30 Ann M. Martin, "My Hometown Library," Ann M. Martin: Letters from Ann, *www.scholastic.com/annmartin/letters/online092304.htm*.

31 R. and Martin, Ann M. Martin: *The Story of the Author of The Baby-sitters Club*, 86.

32 Ibid., 108.

33 Ibid., 109.

34 Ibid., 121.

35 Quoted in Ann Cammire, ed., "Ann M. Martin," *Children's Literature Review*, 200.

36 Ibid.

37 R. and Martin, *Ann M. Martin: The Story of the Author of The Baby-sitters Club*, 134.

38 Schools around the United States, "Ann Martin Interview," *www.hipark.austin.isd.tenet.edu/grade3/hunt/interviewam.htm*.

39 Quoted in Ann Cammire, ed., *Something about the Author* Vol. 44, 117.

40 Leonard S. Marcus, ed., *Author Talk* (New York, NY: Simon and Schuster, 2000), 69.

41 McMurran, "Ann Martin Stirs Up a Tiny Tempest in Preteen Land with her Best-selling Baby-sitters Club," 55.

42 Ferraro, "Girl Talk," 62.

43 R. and Martin, *Ann M. Martin: The Story of the Author of The Baby-sitters Club*, 138.

44 "Transcript of Live Chat With Ann M. Martin," Contemporary Authors Online: May 16, 1989 (Detroit, MI: Gale Group, 2000).

45 Ann M. Martin, "Ann's Mailbag," Ann M. Martin: Letters from Ann, *www.scholastic.com/annmartin/letters/online080603.htm*.

46 Sally Lodge, "Another Busy Season for Ann M. Martin," *Publishers Weekly*, September 1, 1997, 31.

47 Ibid.

48 Ibid.

49 Wendy Cole, "Wake-Up Call," *Time*, June 11, 1990, 75.

50 Martin, *Graduation Day*, 183.

51 Quoted in Ann Cammire, ed., "Ann M. Martin," *Children's Literature Review*, 194.

52 Ferraro, "Girl Talk," 62.

53 Ibid.

54 Ibid.

55 McMurran, "Ann Martin Stirs Up a Tiny Tempest in Preteen Land with her Best-selling Baby-sitters Club," 55.

56 Ferraro, "Girl Talk," 63.

57 "Transcript of Live Chat With Ann M. Martin."

58 Linda Castellitto, "A Special Interview with Ann M. Martin." Booksense.com, *www.booksense.com/people/annmartin.jsp*.

59 Ann M. Martin, "Here Today," Ann M. Martin: Letters from Ann, *www.scholastic.com/annmartin/letters/online022305.htm*.

60 "The Doll People Book Review," *Publishers Weekly*, July 3, 2000.

61 Katherine Devine, "The Meanest Doll in the World," *School Library Journal*, March 2000.

62 Lauralyn Persson, "Pre-School and Primary Grades Fiction," *School Library Journal*, November 1996, 88.

63 R. and Martin, *Ann M. Martin: The Story of the Author of The Baby-sitters Club*, 131.

64 Quoted in Ann Cammire, ed., *Something about the Author* Vol. 44, 117.

65 Marcus, *Author Talk*, 69.

66 American Library Association, "The Newbery Medal," *http://ils.unc.edu/award/nhome.html*.

67 Ibid.

68 Ann M. Martin, "Newbery Honor," Ann M. Martin: Letters from Ann, *www.scholastic.com/annmartin/letters/online031503.htm*.

69 Lynda Brill Comerford, "PWW Talks with Ann M. Martin," *Publishers Weekly*, July 22, 2002, 181.

70 Schools around the United States, "Ann Martin Interview," *www.hipark.austin.isd.tenet.edu/grade3/hunt/interviewam.htm*.

71 Comerford, "PWW Talks with Ann M. Martin," 181.

72 Martin, "Newbery Honor."

73 Lynda Brill Comerford. "A True Test of Friendship." *Publishers Weekly*, March 9, 1998, 26.

74 R. and Martin, *Ann M. Martin: The Story of the Author of The Baby-sitters Club*, 158.

75 Comerford, "A True Test of Friendship," 26.

76 "The Paula Danziger and Ann M. Martin Interview" Paula Danziger and Ann Martin—Interview, *http://hosted.ukoln.ac.uk/stories/stories/danziger/interview.htm*.

77 "Author Profile: Paula Danziger," Teenreads.com, *www.teenreads.com/authors/au-danziger-paula.asp*.

78 "The Paula Danziger and Ann M. Martin Interview."

79 Ron Koertge, "Please Mr. Postman," *The New York Times Book Review*, May 17, 1998, 27.

80 Michael Cart, "Books for Youth: Books for Middle Readers," *Booklist*, March 15, 2000, 1376.

81 Ann Elders, "Review of Snail Mail No More," *School Library Journal*, March 2001, 88.

82 "The Paula Danziger and Ann M. Martin Interview."

83 Ann M. Martin, "Good-bye to Summer, Hello to Fall," Letters from Ann, *www.scholastic.com/annmartin/letters/online102104.htm.*

84 Castellitto, "A Special Interview with Ann M. Martin."

85 R. and Martin, *Ann M. Martin: The Story of the Author of The Baby-sitters Club,* 162.

86 Ingrid Chevanne, "Ann Martin Tour Teaches Fans to Volunteer," *Publishers Weekly,* May 17, 1999, 34.

87 Ann M. Martin, "Bringing Books to Children," Scholastic Books website, *www.scholastic.com/annmartin/index.htm.*

88 Ann M. Martin, "The Lisa Libraries," Letters from Ann, *www.scholastic.com/annmartin/letters/online3_20_00.htm.*

89 Ferraro, "Girl Talk," 63.

90 Quoted in Ann Cammire, ed., *Something about the Author* Vol. 44, 117.

91 R. and Martin, *Ann M. Martin: The Story of the Author of The Baby-sitters Club,* 7.

92 Ibid., 154.

93 Ibid., 164.

1955 Ann Mathews Martin is born during hurricane Connie on August 12 in Princeton, New Jersey.

1957 Jane Martin, Ann's younger sister, is born.

1966 Martin falls while climbing down a tree house; she undergoes surgery to remove her spleen.

1970–1973 Martin begins volunteering at the Eden Institute during the summer months.

1973 Martin graduates from Princeton High School with honors.

1973–1977 Martin attends Smith College in Northampton, Massachusetts.

1977 Martin graduates from Smith College with honors and starts teaching at Plumfield School in Noroton, Connecticut.

1979 Martin leaves teaching to work as an editorial assistant for Archway Paperbacks, an imprint of Pocket Books in New York.

1980 Martin leaves Archway Paperbacks and begins her career at Scholastic Book Services as a copywriter; she works her way up to a position as an editor.

1983 Martin's first book, *Bummer Summer*, is published; she becomes senior editor at Bantam Books, Inc.

1985 Martin becomes a full-time writer; she is asked to write books for a new series: the Baby-sitters Club.

1986 The first Baby-sitters Club book, *Kristy's Great Idea*, is published.

1988 *Baby-sitters On Board!*, the first Baby-sitters Club Super Special book, is published; *Karen's Witch*, the first Little Sisters book, is published.

1990 *Karen's Wish*, the first Little Sisters Super Special book, is published.

1991 *Stacey and the Missing Ring*, the first Baby-sitters Club Mystery book, is published.

1993 *Dawn's Book*, the first Baby-sitters Club Portrait Collection book, is published; *Logan Bruno, Boy Baby-sitter*, the first Baby-sitters Club Special Editions book, is published.

1995   *Baby-sitters Haunted House*, the first Baby-sitters Club Super Mysteries book, is published.

1996   *Leo the Magnificat* is published; *Teacher's Pet*, the first The Kids in Ms. Coleman's Class book, is published.

1997   *Dawn*, the first California Diaries book, is published.

1999   *Kristy's Big News*, the first Friends Forever book is published; *Everything Changes*, the first Friends Forever Special book, is published.

2000   Martin and Scholastic Books stop writing and publishing the Baby-sitters Club books and all spin-off series books.

2003   Martin's book, *A Corner of the Universe*, receives a Newbery Honor.

2004   *Here Today* is published.

2005   Martin continues to write and anticipates the release of two books, *The Runaway Dolls* and *A Dog's Life* in 2005.

BELLE TEAL

This middle grade novel started out as a short story that Ann M. Martin wrote to be included in a collection of short stories written by Smith College alumni. *Belle Teal* gives young readers an eye-opening view of desegregation, a milestone in Civil Rights history that Martin did not personally experience, but remembers and thoroughly researched in order to inform young readers.

BUMMER SUMMER

Bummer Summer was Ann M. Martin's first middle-grade-fiction novel. The protagonist, 12-year-old Kammy Whitlock, faces two conflicts simultaneously: her widowed father's remarriage and her first experience at sleep-away summer camp. *Bummer Summer* received mixed reviews from the press, but it was voted by young readers to the Children's Choice List for 1985. Martin also received a New Jersey Author Award from the New Jersey Institute of Technology in 1983, for *Bummer Summer*.

A CORNER OF THE UNIVERSE

A Corner of the Universe is Ann M. Martin's most biographical novel. It is based on events that occurred in her mother's family before Martin was born. The story, which is set during the summer of 1960, is told from the view point of a young girl, Hattie Owens, who expects her summer to be filled with helping her mother run the family's boarding house, painting alongside her artist father, and reading a multitude of books. Then Uncle Adam, a mentally ill uncle Hattie did not know existed, arrives and turns her world upside down. *A Corner of the Universe* won a Newbery Honor award in 2003.

THE DOLL PEOPLE

In this fantasy, co-written with Laura Godwin and illustrated by Brian Selznick, Ann M. Martin steps away from the tough realistic issues that she writes about in many of her other novels. The main characters of *The Doll People* are dolls—the antique, highly prized Annabelle Doll, and the modern, plastic Tiffany Funcraft. The worlds of these two dolls collide when they both find themselves living in Nora and Kate Palmer's house. Martin and Godwin continued the stories of *The Doll People* with *The Meanest Doll in the World* and *The Runaway Dolls*.

INSIDE OUT

Ann M. Martin tackled autism in *Inside Out*, a middle-grade novel published in 1984. *Inside Out* is one of the two books written by

Martin narrated from a boy's point of view—the other is *Ma and Pa Dracula*. Jonno is 11 years old and his brother James is autistic. Martin realistically portrays the tension-filled home and does not promise that James will ever lead a normal life. The subject of autism in a middle-grade novel was relatively new back in 1984, and Martin relied heavily on her work with autistic children at the Eden Institute in New Jersey for the novel's content. *Inside Out* was a Child Study Association of America's Children's Books of the Year selection in 1986.

KRISTY'S GREAT IDEA

Kristy's Great Idea, the first book in the Baby-sitters Club series, begins with Kristy Thomas's idea to start a baby-sitters club. Ann M. Martin introduces the four pre-teenage girls—Kristy, Mary Anne Spier, Claudia Kishi, and Stacey McGill—who form the club. Their names have become synonymous with the Baby-sitters Club books—a series that was added to for almost 15 years until the series was discontinued in 2000.

HERE TODAY

Here Today is the third of Ann M. Martin's novels to take place in the 1960s. It is set against the historical events surrounding President John F. Kennedy's assassination. As she has done with many of her earlier books, Martin tells the story from the point of view of a pre-adolescent girl who is struggling to overcome a personal challenge. In this case, the challenge is that her mother has abandoned her.

MA AND PA DRACULA

Ann M. Martin demonstrates her multiple writing talents in this fantasy, *Ma and Pa Dracula*, which was published in 1989. One of the two books by the author written from a boy's point of view— the other is *Inside Out*—Martin writes of fourth grader, Jonathan Primave's attempts to live a normal life, knowing he has been adopted by vampires. The book is part silly and part gruesome, but throughout the message is clear: loving someone means doing what is best for him or her.

MARY ANNE AND THE MEMORY GARDEN

Mary Anne and the Memory Garden is one of the Baby-sitters Club books. It was written by Ann M. Martin in 1995 in response to the many readers who wrote to her asking her for a book that dealt with the death of a friend. In the story, Mary Anne's friend Amelia is killed by a drunk driver. Mary Anne gets help with dealing with

Amelia's death from a psychiatrist, and finds a special way to honor her friend's memory.

MISSING SINCE MONDAY

Teenager Maggie Ellis and her brother Mark are put in charge of their 4-year-old stepsister Courtenay in *Missing Since Monday*, published in 1986. *Missing Since Monday* is as suspenseful as it is informative. As it becomes clear that Courtenay has been kidnapped, Martin uses the plot as a venue for dispensing valuable information about how a search for a missing child is undertaken. *Missing Since Monday* received a Child Study Association of America's Children's Books of the Year selection in 1987.

P.S. LONGER LETTER LATER

Ann M. Martin collaborated with her good friend, the late Paula Danziger to write *P.S. Longer Letter Later*, a book made up of letters. Each author assumed the role of one of the book's characters: Martin was reserved Elizabeth and Danziger was Tara*Starr. The girls are best friends despite their differences and when Tara*Starr moves to Ohio, they are determined not to let distance end their friendship. The two authors followed up *P.S. Longer Letter Later* with a sequel *Snail Mail, No More* in which the friends' letters are e-mails.

TEN KIDS, NO PETS

There is a whole host of characters in *Ten Kids, No Pets*—the entire Rosso clan. In 1995, Ann M. Martin wrote this hilarious book about a family of 12 that moves from the city to the country. Some reviewers felt that with so many characters, it was difficult to get to know them all, but it is easy to see that all 10 children want one thing: a pet. Mrs. Rosso's mantra of "ten kids are enough—no pets" takes on an entirely different meaning when the family learns that an 11th child is on the way. Martin followed up *Ten Kids, No Pets* with the sequel, *Eleven Kids, One Summer*.

YOURS TURLY, SHIRLEY

Ann M. Martin addressed the learning disability, dyslexia in *Yours Turly, Shirley*, written in 1988. Martin contrasts Shirley Basini's dyslexia with Shirley's 8-year-old sister Jacki, who is adopted from Vietnam and who, with Shirley's help, becomes a better reader than Shirley. For a while, the competition between the two sisters appears to derail Shirley's hard work to overcome her disability, but in the end, Shirley emerges the victor, giving hope to all children suffering from dyslexia who read this book.

WITH YOU AND WITHOUT YOU

Ann M. Martin tackled another tough subject—grief and adjustment to the loss of a parent—in *With You and Without You*, published in 1986. In this book, Liza O'Hara's father dies and Liza must come to terms with his death along with the many changes it brings to her family. The theme of the book—that life does go on "with or without you" made it a book of choice among counselors helping children coping with the death of a loved one. It received a Child Study Association of America's Children's Books of the Year selection in 1987.

1983 *Bummer Summer*; *Just You and Me*; *My Puppy Scrapbook* (written with Betsy Ryan)

1984 *Inside Out*; *Stage Fright*

1985 *Me and Katie (the Pest)*

1986 *With You and Without You*; *Missing Since Monday*

1987 *Just a Summer Romance*; *Slam Book*

1988 *Yours Turly, Shirley*; *Ten Kids, No Pets*; *Fancy Dance in Feather Town*

1989 *Ma and Pa Dracula*; *Moving Day in Feather Town*

1991 *Eleven Kids, One Summer*

1992 *Enchanted Attic*; *Rachel Parker, Kindergarten Show-off*

1993 *Chain Letter*; *Ann M. Martin: The Story of the Author of the Baby-Sitters Club*

1996 *Leo the Magnificat*

1998 *P.S. Longer Letter Later* (written with Paula Danziger)

1999 *The Doll People* (written with Laura Godwin)

2000 *Snail Mail No More* (written with Paula Danziger)

2001 *Belle Teal*

2002 *A Corner of the Universe*

2003 *The Meanest Doll in the World* (written with Laura Godwin)

2004 *Here Today*

2005 *The Runaway Dolls* (written with Laura Godwin); *A Dog's Life*

BABY-SITTERS CLUB SERIES

1986 *Kristy's Great Idea*; *Claudia and the Phantom Phone Calls*; *The Truth about Stacey*

1987 *Mary Anne Saves the Day*; *Dawn and the Impossible Three*; *Kristy's Big Day*; *Claudia and Mean Janine*; *Boy-Crazy Stacey*

1988 *The Ghost at Dawn's House*; *Logan Likes Mary Anne!*; *Kristy and the Snobs*; *Claudia and the New Girl*; *Good-bye Stacey, Good-bye*; *Hello, Mallory*; *Little Miss Stoneybrook . . . and Dawn*; *Jessi's Secret Language*; *Mary Anne's Bad-Luck Mystery*; *Stacey's Mistake*; *Dawn on the Coast*; *Claudia and the Bad Joke*

1989 *Kristy and the Walking Disaster*; *Mallory and the Trouble with the Twins*; *Jessi Ramsey, Pet-Sitter*; *Kristy and the Mother's Day Surprise*; *Mary Anne and the Search for Tigger*; *Claudia and the*

Sad Good-bye; *Jessi and the Superbrat*; *Welcome Back, Stacey!*; *Mallory and the Mystery Diary*

1990 *Mary Anne and the Great Romance*; *Dawn's Wicked Stepsister*; *Kristy and the Secret of Susan*; *Claudia and the Great Search*; *Mary Anne and Too Many Boys*; *Stacey and the Mystery of Stoneybrook*; *Jessi's Baby-Sitter*; *Dawn and the Older Boy*; *Kristy's Mystery Admirer*; *Poor Mallory*; *Claudia and the Middle School Mystery*; *Mary Anne vs. Logan*

1991 *Jessi and the Dance School Phantom*; *Stacey's Emergency*; *Dawn and the Big Sleepover*; *Kristy and the Baby Parade*; *Mary Anne Misses Logan*; *Mallory on Strike*; *Jessi's Wish*; *Claudia and the Genius of Elm Street*

1992 *Dawn's Big Date*; *Stacey's Ex-Best Friend*; *Mary Anne and Too Many Babies*; *Kristy for President*; *Mallory and the Dream Horse*; *Jessi's Gold Medal*; *Keep out, Claudia!*; *Dawn Saves the Planet*; *Stacey's Choice*; *Mallory Hates Boys (and Gym)*

1993 *Mary Anne's Makeover*; *Jessi and the Awful Secret*; *Kristy and the Worst Kid Ever*; *Claudia's Friend*; *Dawn's Family Feud*; *Stacey's Big Crush*; *Maid Mary Anne*; *Dawn's Big Move*; *Jessi and the Bad Baby-Sitter*; *Get Well Soon, Mallory*; *Stacey and the Cheerleaders*

1994 *Claudia and the Perfect Boy*; *Dawn and the We Love Kids Club*; *Mary Anne and Miss Priss*; *Kristy and the Copycat*; *Jessi's Horrible Prank*; *Stacey's Lie*; *Dawn and Whitney, Friends Forever*; *Claudia and Crazy Peaches*; *Mary Anne Breaks the Rules*; *Mallory Pike, #1 Fan*

1995 *Kristy and Mr. Mom*; *Jessi and the Troublemaker*; *Stacey vs. the BSC*; *Dawn and the School Spirit War*; *Claudia Kishi, Live from WSTO*; *Mary Anne and Camp BSC*; *Stacey and the Bad Girls*; *Farewell, Dawn*; *Kristy and the Dirty Diapers*; *Welcome to the BSC, Abby*; *Claudia and the First Thanksgiving*; *Mallory's Christmas Wish*

1996 *Mary Anne and the Memory Garden*; *Stacey McGill, Super Sitter*; *Kristy + Bart = ?*; *Abby's Lucky Thirteen*; *Claudia and the World's Cutest Baby*; *Dawn and Too Many Sitters*; *Stacey's Broken Heart*; *Kristy's Worst Idea*; *Claudia Kishi, Middle School Drop Out*; *Mary Anne and the Little Princess*; *Happy Holidays, Jessi*

1997 *Abby's Twin*; *Stacey the Match Whiz*; *Claudia, Queen of the Seventh Grade*; *Mind Your Own Business, Kristy!*; *Don't Give up,*

Mallory; Mary Anne to the Rescue; Abby the Bad Sport; Stacey's Secret Friend; Kristy and the Sister War; Claudia Makes up Her Mind; The Secret Life of Mary Anne Spier; Jessi's Big Break; Abby and the Best Kid Ever; Claudia and the Terrible Truth; Kristy Thomas, Dog Trainer; Stacey's Ex-Boyfriend; Mary Anne and the Playground Fight; Abby in Wonderland; Kristy in Charge

1998 *Claudia's Big Party; Stacey McGill . . . Matchmaker?; Mary Anne in the Middle; The All-New Mallory Pike; Abby's Un-Valentine*

1999 *Claudia and the Little Liar; Kristy at Bat; Stacey's Movie; The Fire at Mary Anne's House*

2000 *Graduation Day*

BABY-SITTERS CLUB FRIENDS FOREVER SERIES

1999 *Kristy's Big News; Stacey vs. Claudia; Mary Anne's Big Break Up; Claudia and the Friendship Feud; Kristy Power; Stacey and the Boyfriend Trap*

2000 *Claudia Gets Her Guy; Mary Anne's Revenge; Kristy and the Kidnapper; Stacey's Problem; Welcome Home, Mary Anne; Claudia and the Disaster Date*

BABY-SITTERS CLUB FRIENDS FOREVER SPECIAL SERIES

1999 *Everything Changes; Graduation Day*

BABY-SITTERS CLUB MYSTERY SERIES

1991 *Stacey and the Missing Ring; Beware, Dawn!*

1992 *Mallory and the Ghost Cat; Kristy and the Missing Child; Mary Anne and the Secret in the Attic; The Mystery at Claudia's House*

1993 *Dawn and the Disappearing Dogs; Jessi and the Jewel Thieves; Kristy and the Haunted Mansion; Stacey and the Mystery Money; Claudia and the Mystery at the Museum; Dawn and the Surfer Ghost; Mary Anne and the Library Mystery*

1994 *Stacey and the Mystery at the Mall; Kristy and the Vampires; Claudia and the Clue in the Photograph; Dawn and the Halloween Mystery; Stacey and the Mystery at the Empty House*

1995 *Kristy and the Missing Fortune; Mary Anne and the Zoo Mystery; Claudia and the Recipe for Danger; Stacey and the Haunted Masquerade*

1996 *Abby and the Secret Society; Mary Anne and the Silent Witness; Kristy and the Middle School Vandal; Dawn Schafer, Undercover Baby-Sitter; Claudia and the Lighthouse Ghost*

1997 *Abby and the Mystery Baby; Stacey and the Fashion Victim; Kristy and the Mystery Train; Mary Anne and the Music Box Secret; Claudia and the Mystery in the Painting; Stacey and the Stolen Hearts; Mary Anne and the Haunted Bookstore; Abby and the Notorious Neighbor; Kristy and the Cat Burglar*

BABY-SITTERS CLUB SUPER SPECIALS SERIES

1988 *Baby-Sitters on Board!*

1989 *Baby-Sitters Summer Vacation; Baby-Sitters Winter Vacation*

1990 *Baby-Sitters Island Adventure; California Girls!*

1991 *New York, New York!; Snowbound*

1992 *Baby-Sitters at Shadow Lake; Starring the Baby-Sitters Club*

1993 *Sea City, Here We Come!*

1994 *The Baby-Sitters Remember; Here Come the Bridesmaids!*

1996 *Aloha, Baby-Sitters!*

BABY-SITTERS LITTLE SISTER SERIES

1988 *Karen's Witch; Karen's Roller Skates*

1989 *Karen's Worst Day; Karen's Kittycat Club; Karen's School Picture; Karen's Little Sister*

1990 *Karen's Birthday; Karen's Haircut; Karen's Sleepover; Karen's Grandmothers; Karen's Prize; Karen's Ghost; Karen's Surprise*

1991 *Karen's New Year; Karen's in Love; Karen's Goldfish; Karen's Brothers; Karen's Home Run; Karen's Good-Bye; Karen's Carnival; Karen's New Teacher*

1992 *Karen's Little Witch; Karen's Doll; Karen's School Trip; Karen's Pen Pal; Karen's Ducklings; Karen's Big Joke; Karen's Tea Party; Karen's Cartwheel; Karen's Kittens; Karen's Bully; Karen's Pumpkin Patch; Karen's Secret*

1993 *Karen's Snow Day; Karen's Doll Hospital; Karen's New Friend; Karen's Tuba; Karen's Big Lie; Karen's Wedding; Karen's School; Karen's Pizza Party; Karen's Toothache; Karen's Big Weekend*

1994 *Karen's Twin; Karen's Baby-Sitter; Karen's Kite; Karen's Two Families; Karen's Stepmother; Karen's Lucky Penny; Karen's Big*

Top; *Karen's Mermaid*; *Karen's School Bus*; *Karen's Candy*; *Karen's Magician*; *Karen's Ice Skates*

1995 *Karen's School Mystery*; *Karen's Ski Trip*; *Karen's Leprechaun*; *Karen's Pony*; *Karen's Tattletale*; *Karen's New Bike*; *Karen's Movie*; *Karen's Lemonade Stand*; *Karen's Toys*; *Karen's Monsters*; *Karen's Turkey Day*; *Karen's Angel*

1996 *Karen's Big Sister*; *Karen's Grandad*; *Karen's Island Adventure*; *Karen's New Puppy*; *Karen's Dinosaur*; *Karen's Softball Mystery*; *Karen's County Fair*; *Karen's Magic Garden*; *Karen's School Surprise*; *Karen's Half Birthday*; *Karen's Big Fight*; *Karen's Christmas Tree*; *Karen's Accident*

1997 *Karen's Secret Valentine*; *Karen's Bunny*; *Karen's Big Job*; *Karen's Treasure*; *Karen's Telephone Trouble*; *Karen's Pony Camp*; *Karen's Puppet Show*; *Karen's Unicorn, Scholastic, Inc.*; *Karen's Haunted House*; *Karen's Pilgrim*; *Karen's Sleigh Ride*; *Karen's Cooking Contest*; *Karen's Snow Princess*; *Karen's Promise*; *Karen's Big Move*; *Karen's Paper Route*; *Karen's Fishing Trip*; *Karen's Big City Mystery*; *Karen's Book*; *Karen's Chain Letter*; *Karen's Black Cat*; *Karen's Movie Star*; *Karen's Christmas Carol*

1998 *Karen's Nanny*; *Karen's President*; *Karen's Copycat*; *Karen's Field Day*; *Karen's Show and Share*; *Karen's Swim Meet*; *Karen's Spy Mystery*; *Karen's New Holiday*; *Karen's Hurricane*

1999 *Karen's Chicken Pox*; *Karen's Runaway Turkey*; *Karen's Reindeer*

2000 *Karen's Mistake*; *Karen's Figure Eight*; *Karen's Yo-Yo*; *Karen's Easter Parade*; *Karen's Gift*; *Karen's Cowboy*

BABY-SITTERS LITTLE SISTERS SUPER SPECIAL SERIES

1990 *Karen's Wish*

1991 *Karen's Plane Trip*; *Karen's Mystery*

1992 *Karen, Hannie, and Nancy: The Three Musketeers*; *Karen's Baby*

1993 *Karen's Campout*

BABY-SITTERS CLUB PORTRAIT COLLECTION SERIES

1993 *Dawn's Book*

1994 *Stacey's Book*

1995 *Claudia's Book*

1996 *Mary Anne's Book; Kristy's Book*

1997 *Abby's Book*

BABY-SITTERS CLUB SUPER MYSTERIES SPECIAL

1995 *Baby-sitters' Haunted House; Baby-sitters Beware*

1996 *Baby-Sitters' Fright Night*

BABY-SITTERS CLUB SPECIAL EDITIONS

1993 *Logan Bruno; Baby-Sitters Little Sister School Scrapbook; Baby-Sitters Club Guide to Baby-sitting*

1994 *Shannon's Story; Secret Santa*

1995 *Baby-Sitters Little Sister Summer Fill-in Book; Baby-Sitters Little Sister Jump Rope Rhymes*

1996 *Baby-Sitters Little Sister Playground Games; Complete Guide to the Baby-Sitters Club; The BSC Notebook; BSC Chain Letter; The Baby-Sitters Club Trivia and Puzzle Fun Book; The Baby-Sitters Club Postcard Book*

1997 *Little Sister Photo Scrapbook; Baby-Sitters Little Sister Secret Diary; Baby-Sitters Little Sister Laugh Pack*

THE KIDS IN MS. COLMAN'S CLASS SERIES

1996 *Teacher's Pet; Author Day; Class Play; The Second Grade Baby*

1997 *Snow War; Twin Trouble; Science Fair; Summer Kids*

1998 *Halloween Parade; Holiday Time; Spelling Bee; Baby Animal Zoo*

CALIFORNIA DIARIES SERIES

1997 *Dawn; Sunny; Maggie; Amalia; Ducky*

1998 *Dawn Diary Two; Sunny Diary Two; Maggie Diary Two; Amalia Diary Two; Ducky Diary Two*

1999 *Dawn Diary Three; Sunny Diary Three*

2000 *Maggie Diary Three; Amalia Diary Three*

2001 *Ducky Diary Three*

KAMMY WHITLOCK

The protagonist of *Bummer Summer*, 12-year-old Kammy Whitlock's mother died when Kammy was 4 years old. For eight years Kammy and her father live a comfortable life, but when he marries a woman who is 19 years younger than he, Kammy has to deal with a 3-year-old stepsister and a baby stepbrother. She thinks her father and stepmother are just trying to get rid of her for the summer when they suggest summer camp, but the experience teaches her the true meaning of family.

LIZA O'HARA

Twelve-year-old Lizzie O'Hara is part of a warm and close-knit family in *With You and Without You*. When her father dies of heart disease, at first Liza is angry that other members of her family seem to be able to have a good time while she is in mourning. Eventually she comes to understand how to come to terms with her father's death, and in doing so, learns that everyone grieves in his or her own way.

HATTIE OWEN

Hattie Owen is the one Ann M. Martin character most like Martin herself. The book Hattie appears in, *A Corner of the Universe*, is based in part upon events that happened in Martin's own family. Hattie, a shy, 11-year-old, only child, is just beginning her summer vacation. With her one friend away for the summer, Hattie expects the months to pass uneventfully, built upon routine and filled with books. When her parents tell her that she has an uncle who she has never heard of, she is shocked that they have kept him a secret. Uncle Adam is mentally-ill and Hattie's summer plans shift as he arrives and she must fill an ever changing roll: niece, baby-sitter, friend, and protector. It is in coming to understand and love him that Hattie comes to know and accept herself.

ANNABELLE DOLL

Annabelle is a beautiful antique doll who has been handed down from generation to generation in the Palmer family for over 100 years. Now she is owned by Kate Palmer. Annabelle and the rest of her doll family are able to come to life, although if they are seen by a human, they risk "permanent doll state." Annabelle comes from a family that is prim and proper, although they do like to sing songs from the 1960s like "Respect." When the pink, plastic Tiffany Funcraft doll moves into the bedroom next door, Annabelle's world starts spinning out of control.

BELLE TEAL HARPER

Belle Teal Harper, the protagonist in *Belle Teal* lost her father when she was a baby. Her mother and grandmother are the only family she has ever known. As she enters fifth grade at Coker Creek Elementary School, she is confronted with her grandmother's increasing forgetfulness and her mother's return to school so that she can find a better job. Belle is the only one in her class brave enough to befriend an African-American boy who, because of desegregation, now goes to Belle's school. Belle's skillful juggling of all these issues makes her appear wise beyond her years.

ELLIE DINGMAN

Ellie Dingman, the 11-year-old main character of *Here Today* has two main conflicts to resolve. First, her mother wants to be a movie star more than she wants to be a mother (her children call her by her first name, Doris), and second, Ellie must deal with the way her schoolmates treat her and the other children from her neighborhood—as though they are freaks. In both situations, Ellie emerges with newfound strength that amazes even her.

ELIZABETH AND TARA*STARR

Elizabeth and Tara*Starr are pen pals in Ann M. Martin's collaborations with the late Paula Danziger: *P.S. Longer Letter Later* and *Snail Mail No More*. Elizabeth is shy and reserved; her favorite hobby is the solitary act of knitting. Elizabeth's family seems to be solid until her father loses his job and has a nervous breakdown. Tara*Starr is whimsical, colorful, and glitzy. Her parents move to Ohio and her mother soon becomes pregnant. Elizabeth and Tara*Starr, although they seem to be complete opposites of one another, maintain their friendship first through letters (which make up *P.S. Longer Letter Later*) and later email (documented in *Snail Mail No More*), proving that the bonds of friendship are stronger than distance or differences in personality.

KRISTIN AMANDA THOMAS

Kristy is the originator and president of the Baby-sitters Club. She is feisty, outspoken, impulsive, and more than a little bossy. Kristy does not care much for clothes; she often looks and dresses like a tomboy. She loves animals and sports. Her best friend is Mary Ann Spier who lives across the street. Kristy's parents are divorced, and she lives with one younger and two older brothers.

CLAUDIA LYNN KISHI

Claudia is the vice president of the Baby-sitters Club and the club meets at her house because she has a phone in her room. She is Japanese American and her two passions are art and reading mysteries. She loves using her clothes and accessories to make a statement. Claudia eats tons of junk food, which she keeps stashed away in her room. She has an older sister named Janine, who is a genius.

MARY ANNE SPIER

Mary Anne is the girl in the Baby-sitters Club most like Ann M. Martin. She is a shy, only-child whose mother died when she was very young. Mary Anne has been raised by her dad, who is strict and expects a lot from her. Perhaps because of this, she is organized and a good manager. Mary Anne serves as secretary for the Baby-sitters Club. Her boyfriend is the club's first boy baby-sitter, Logan Bruno.

STACEY (ANASTASIA) MCGILL

Stacey is an only child. Her family moves from New York City to Stonybrook where she becomes Claudia's best friend and joins the Baby-sitters Club as the club's treasurer. She loves to shop, is a trendy dresser, and creates a sensation wherever she goes; sometimes Stacey's glamorous and sophisticated looks are overshadowed by her battle with diabetes, which is featured in many of the Baby-sitters Club books.

1983 *Bummer Summer*, awarded New Jersey Author by the New Jersey Institute of Technology.

1985 *Bummer Summer*, awarded Children's Choice Award.

1986 *Inside Out*, included on the Child Study Association of America's Children's Books of the Year list.

1987 *Missing Since Monday*, awarded New Jersey Author by the New Jersey Institute of Technology. *Inside Out, Stage Fright, With You and Without You,* and *Missing Since Monday,* included on the Child Study Association of America's Children's Books of the Year list.

1998 *Leo the Magnificat*, awarded Keystone State Reading Award.

2000 *P.S. Longer Letter Later*, nominated for the California Young Reader Medal.

2001 *P.S. Longer Letter Later*, nominated for the Washington Sasquatch Reading Award.

2003 *A Corner of the Universe*, awarded Newbery honor book by the American Library Assocation.

American Library Association, "The Newbery Medal," *http://ils.unc.edu/award/nhome.html.*

"Author Profile: Paula Danziger." Teenreads.com, *www.teenreads.com/authors/au-danziger-paula.asp.*

R., Margot Becker, and Ann M. Martin. *Ann M. Martin: The Story of the Author of the Baby-sitters Club.* New York, NY: Scholastic Inc., 1993.

Brachmann, Kathleen. "A Review of Bummer Summer." *School Library Journal* Vol. 29, No. 1, August, 1983.

Cammire, Ann, ed. "Ann M. Martin." *Children's Literature Review* Vol. 32. Detroit, MI: Gale Research, 1986.

———. *Something about the Author* Vol. 44. Detroit, MI: Gale Research, 1986.

Cart, Michael. "Books for Youth: Books for Middle Readers." *Booklist,* March 15, 2000.

Castellitto, Linda. "A Special Interview with Ann M. Martin." Booksense.com, *www.booksense.com/people/annmartin.jsp.*

Chevanne, Ingrid. "Ann Martin Tour Teaches Fans to Volunteer." *Publishers Weekly*, May 17, 1999.

Cole, Wendy. "Wake-Up Call," *Time*, June 11, 1990.

Comerford, Lynda Brill. "A True Test of Friendship." *Publishers Weekly*, March 9, 1998.

———. "PWW Talks with Ann M. Martin." *Publishers Weekly*, July 22, 2002.

Devine, Katherine. "The Meanest Doll in the World." *School Library Journal*, March 2000.

"The Doll People Book Review," *Publishers Weekly,* July 3, 2000.

Elders, Ann. "Review of Snail Mail No More," *School Library Journal*, March 2001.

Ferraro, Susan. "Girl Talk." *New York Times*, December 5, 1992.

Henneman, Heidi. "Bye-bye to The Baby-Sitters Club," BookPage Interview January 2001: Ann Martin, *www.bookpage.com/0101bp/ann_martin.html.*

Holtze, Sally Holmes, ed. *Seventh Book of Junior Authors and Illustrators*. Bronx, NY: The H.W. Wilson Company, 1996.

Kleinfield, N.R. "Children's Books: Inside the Baby-Sitters Club." *New York Times Book Review*, April 30, 1989.

Koertge, Ron. "Please Mr. Postman." *The New York Times Book Review*, May 17, 1998.

Lodge, Sally. "Another Busy Season for Ann M. Martin." *Publishers Weekly*, September 1, 1997.

MacKey, Margaret. "Filling the Gaps: 'The Baby-Sitters Club,' the Series Book, and the Learning Reader." *Language Arts* Vol. 67, No. 5, September, 1990.

Marcus, Leonard S., ed. *Author Talk*. New York, NY: Simon and Schuster, 2000.

Martin, Ann M. "Ann M. Martin's Biography." Scholastic.com | AuthorsandBooks: Author Booklist, *www2.scholastic.com/teachers/authorsandbooks/authorstudies/authorhome.jhtml?authorID=57&collateralID=5225&displayName=Biography*.

————. "Ann's Mailbag," Ann M. Martin: Letters from Ann, *www.scholastic.com/annmartin/letters/online080603.htm*.

————. "Bringing Books to Children," Scholastic Books website, *www.scholastic.com/annmartin/index.htm*.

————. "Fast Facts." Scholastic Canada: Ann Martin, *www.scholastic.ca/authors/martin_a/facts.htm*.

————. "Goodbye BSC!" Ann M. Martin: Letters from Ann, *www.scholastic.com/annmartin/letters/online1200.htm*.

————. "Good-bye to Summer, Hello to Fall," Letters from Ann, *www.scholastic.com/annmartin/letters/online102104.htm*.

————. *Graduation Day*. New York, NY: Scholastic Inc., 2000.

————. "Here Today," Ann M. Martin: Letters from Ann, *www.scholastic.com/annmartin/letters/online022305.htm*.

————. "My Hometown Library," Ann M. Martin: Letters from Ann, *www.scholastic.com/annmartin/letters/online092304.htm*.

————. "Newbery Honor." Ann M. Martin: Letters from Ann, *www.scholastic.com/annmartin/letters/online031503.htm*.

————. "The Lisa Libraries." Letters from Ann, *www.scholastic.com/annmartin/letters/online3_20_00.htm*.

————. "Where do I Get My Ideas?" Ann M. Martin: Letters from Ann, *www.scholastic.com/annmartin/letters/online0301.htm*.

McMurran, Kristin. "Ann Martin Stirs Up a Tiny Tempest in Preteen Land with her Best-selling Baby-sitters Club." *People Weekly*, August 21, 1989.

"The Paula Danziger and Ann M. Martin Interview" Paula Danziger and Ann Martin—Interview, *http://hosted.ukoln.ac.uk/stories/stories/danziger/interview.htm.*

Persson, Lauralyn. "Pre-School and Primary Grades Fiction." *School Library Journal*, November 1996.

Schools around the United States. "Ann Martin Interview," *www.hipark.austin.isd.tenet.edu/grade3/hunt/interviewam.htm.*

Sebesta, Sam Leaton, and James L. Neeley. "Literature for Children." *The Reading Teacher* Vol 42, No 7, March 1989.

Sutherland, Zena. "A Review of Bummer Summer." *Bulletin of the Center of Children's Books* Vol. 36, No 11, July–August, 1983.

"Transcript of Live Chat With Ann M. Martin." Contemporary Authors Online: May 16, 1989, Detroit, MI: Gale Group, 2000.

Clark, Darakjian Arda. *Dyslexia*. Detroit, MI: Thomson-Gale, 2005.

Coville, Bruce. "The Joy of Paula." *The Horn Book Magazine*, September 1, 2004.

Krull, Kathleen. *Presenting Paula Danziger*. Farmington Hills, MI: Twayne Publishers, 1995.

Lennard-Brown, Sarah. *Autism*. Oxford, UK: Raintree, 2003.

Lives and Works: Young Adult Authors. Grolier Academic Reference. Danbury, CT: Grolier Inc., 1998.

Rusch, Elizabeth. *Generation Fix: Young Ideas for a Better World*. Hillsboro, OR: Beyond Words Publishing, 2002.

Somerlott, Robert. *The Little Rock School Desegregation Crisis in American History*. Berkeley Heights, CA: Enslow, 2001.

www.scholastic.com/annmartin/foundation.htm

> *Website of the Ann M. Martin Foundation. Ann M. Martin is the president of this foundation, founded in 1990 to provide financial support to causes benefiting children, education, literacy programs, homeless people, and animals. The site lists how you can contact the foundation.*

www.lisalibraries.org/frames.html

> *Website of the Lisa Libraries. Ann M. Martin and friends started the Lisa Libraries in 1990 to honor and remember children's book editor, Lisa Novak. The goal of the Lisa Libraries is to provide children with books. In 2004, the Lisa Libraries gave over 15,000 books to non-profit organizations across the United States. The site lists how you can contact the Lisa Libraries, donate books, or make monetary gifts.*

www.wish.org

> *Website of Make-A-Wish Foundation. Ann M. Martin supports the Make-A-Wish Foundation, which grants wishes of children who are living with life-threatening medical conditions. The Make-A-Wish Foundation's goal is to bring hope, strength, and joy to these children.*

www.starlight.org/intl/about

> *Website of the Starlight Children's Foundation. Starlight Children's Foundation was founded in 1983 and continues to work to improve the quality of life for seriously ill children and their families. Ann M. Martin supports this international nonprofit organization.*

www.savethechildren.org

> *Website for Save the Children. Ann M. Martin supports Save the Children, an independent organization that works to ensure the well-being of children in more than 100 countries around the world. Save the Children is a member of the International Save the Children Alliance.*

page:

10: © Time Life Pictures/Getty Images

15: © Time Life Pictures/Getty Images

22: © Time Life Pictures/Getty Images

28: © Lee Snider/ Photo Images/CORBIS

36: © James Marshall/CORBIS

39: © Eden Institute, Inc.

46: © Time Life Pictures/ Getty Images

49: © The Cartoon Bank

60: © Dirk Zimmer

66: © Bettmann/CORBIS

74: © AP Photo/Denis Poroy

80: © MCA/Universal Pictures/Getty Images

82: Courtesy of www.boardgamesRus.com

87: © Chelsea House Publishers

90: © Getty Images

95: © Scholastic Inc.

98: © Associated Press, AP/Eric Draper

101: © Time Life Pictures/Getty Images

Cover: © Time Life Pictures/Getty Images

MARYLOU MORANO KJELLE is a freelance writer who lives and works in Central New Jersey. She has written over 20 nonfiction books for young readers, and has co-authored and edited others. She holds a M.S. degree from Rutgers University and she teaches reading and writing at a local community college. Her favorite hobby is cooking, and she has a certificate in culinary arts. This is her fifth Chelsea House book, and her second in the WHO WROTE THAT? series.